TALKS

by
Swami Paramatmananda Puri

Volume 3

Revised Edition 2017

Mata Amritanandamayi Center, San Ramon
California, United States

TALKS

Volume 3 - Revised Edition
by Swami Paramatmananda Puri

Published By:
   Mata Amritanandamayi Center
   P.O. Box 613, San Ramon, CA 94583-0613
   USA
   www.amma.org

Copyright© 2017 by Mata Amritanandamayi Center, California, USA
All rights reserved.
No portion of this book, except for brief review, may be reproduced, stored in a retrieval system or transmitted in any form or by any means—electronic, mechanical, photocopying, recording or otherwise—without permission in writing from the publisher.

First printing by MA Center: November 2017

Address in India:
   Mata Amritanandamayi Mission Trust
   Amritapuri, Kollam Dt.
   Kerala 690546, India
   www.amritapuri.org
   inform@amritapuri.org

Europe: www.amma-europe.org

Preface

To
JAGADGURU
*Sri Mata Amritanandamayi Devi
with deep devotion, respectful regards,
and reverential salutations*

Since 1968, Swami Paramatmananda Puri has lived the life of a renunciate in India, moving there at the age of nineteen, to imbibe the spiritual essence of that great and ancient culture. It has been his good fortune to have kept the company of many saints and sages over the years, culminating in his meeting with his Guru, Mata Amritanandamayi, in 1979. As one of her senior disciples, he was eventually asked to return to the U.S. to serve as head of the first ashram in the West, the Mata Amritanandamayi Center, where he remained in residence since from 1990 until 2001.

Many residents and visitors to the Center have shared that one of the high points in programs there have been Swami is talks, encompassing Amma is teachings, his experiences in India, his understanding of scriptural texts, and his life on the spiritual path. With wit and humour, he has synthesized East and West, and created a forum for spiritual learning for people from all walks of life.

Originally available only on tape, his talks have now been transcribed, with his speaking style preserved as much as possible, making these volumes a treasury of wisdom for years to come.

These talks were recorded over twenty years ago. For this revised edition, Swamiji decided to rewrite the book in a more readable style.

Publisher
Amritapuri, India
August 1, 2017

Contents

Questions & Answers - 1	6
Questions & Answers - 2 & Divine Qualities	40
The Greatness of Sages	70
Patience & Discipline	86
Persistence & Devotion	99
Amma On Advaita	121
The Self is Bliss	132
The World Is Unreal	146
Selfishness	160

Questions & Answers - 1

(Questions put to Swami during Satsang time)

There are an infinite number of *jivas*, individual souls, in the universe, and even if we could count the grains of sand on the beach, they wouldn't equal the number of jivas that are there. When God does something, He does it in a very big way.

We, who are rising and sinking in the ocean of life and death, were at one time inhabiting a minute body, perhaps like an amoeba or a single-celled being, and have somehow evolved to a human form. We did not start out like this. We've already gone through many births. In fact, the very fact that we're human beings in this birth, with some spiritual tendencies, means that we've already travelled a long way in our spiritual evolution back to our source, God.

We should not think that there is still so much farther to go. It has already taken a very long time for us to become humans. Once we are a human, and once we are interested in spiritual things, then, relatively speaking, we are almost there. Even in this life, we could achieve it. That is, for the most part, in our hands. It depends on our intensity. As Amma says, if we want to know what time the bus reaches the destination, it depends if it is an express bus or a local bus. A local one will stop at many places and then only reach the destination. An express one will go directly to the destination. Similarly, our intensity, in large part, determines when we'll reach the goal of union with God.

We all know Amma's lifestyle. What does she do everyday? She is always with a lot of people. She gives darshan to tens of thousands of people in India. In some places, there will be five thousand, ten thousand, or even twenty-five thousand people. Why is she doing this? It is certainly not for any name or fame for herself; it is a tremendous strain on her physical form. Why then does she want to contact as many people as she can? There is a story that may explain the reason.

The Greatness of Satsang

The ancient sage Narada went to Lord Vishnu and said, "Bhagavan, I've heard that the darshan of a mahatma is a very great thing. I want to know what is so great about it."

Bhagavan replied, "There is a birdie about to be born on earth on such and such a tree in such and such a place. Go there and ask it when it is born what the greatness of darshan is?"

So, Narada went down from the higher worlds to the earth using his mystic powers. On reaching the tree, he saw an egg in a nest that was just about to break open. As he stood there and watched, a baby bird hatched out of the egg. Looking at it, he said, "Birdie, what is the greatness of *darshan* (in bird language, of course)?" Hearing that, the birdie looked up at him and immediately died. Narada was shocked. "What did I do? I only asked it one thing and it died!"

Going back to Narayana, he said, "Bhagavan, I didn't get any reply. Not only that; the poor thing died right in front of me!"

Bhagavan said, "All right. Let's try again. There is a calf that is about to be born in such and such a place. Go there and ask it about darshan and surely you'll get your answer."

So he went down again. The calf had just been born and was lying there on the ground. Narada said, "Calf, can you tell me the greatness of darshan? Bhagavan sent me down here to get the answer from you." The calf looked up at Narada and suddenly died.

Narada was obviously very upset. He went back to the Lord and said, "Bhagavan, let's forget about this question. Every time that I ask about darshan, some being dies!"

Bhagavan replied, "Well, let's try just one more time. There is a horse that is going to be born in Benares in the king's palace. It is going to be a beautiful thoroughbred. Go ask that baby horse."

So, out of respect for the Lord, Narada went down to the earth again and the same thing happened. He asked the colt the same question, and it died. Returning to the Lord, he said, "Bhagavan, no answer. I've had enough. I don't want to know what the greatness of darshan is."

The Lord said, "I'm really sorry about that. Maybe if you try just one more time, you'll surely get the answer. There is going to be a prince born to the king of Benares in the same palace. Go ask the question to that baby."

"Bhagavan, please; let's just forget it! If I ask the baby and the baby dies, then the king will surely kill me. I don't want to know the greatness of darshan any more. I shouldn't have asked You. I'm going home!" exclaimed the sage.

Narada has no home; he wanders all over the universe singing the Lord's praises to the tune of his *veena*. Knowing this, Bhagavan said, "You know as well as I do that you have no home, so please listen to Me. This time you'll certainly get an answer; I promise. Now go down and ask."

Sure enough, just as the Lord had told, the baby was born in the king's palace. The king welcomed the great *rishi* into his home, did a *padapuja* to him, and then brought him to see the baby. Narada nervously said, "I want to see the baby alone." When everyone had left the room, he turned to the baby and said, "Baby, please tell me, what is the greatness of darshan?"

The baby looked up at him, and what do you think the baby did? He began to talk. He said, "Narada, you surprise me! Don't you recognize me? Previously, I was a bird, and because of your darshan, I became a calf. Then, because of your darshan in that birth, I became a horse, and because of your darshan in that birth, now I'm a prince, I'm a human being and I have spiritual tendencies, and I'm having your darshan now. In this life, I may even realize God, I may attain Self-realization. That is the greatness of the darshan of a mahatma!"

Perhaps this didn't really happen, but it is a story with a *tattva*, a principle. Amma knows the value of satsang. She knows the value of darshan. If her eyes rest on a soul for a moment, if her breath falls on someone, if we sit in her presence and receive the divine vibrations radiating from her, that will help us evolve.

Most of the people that come to Amma are not doing *sadhana*; they may not even be vaguely interested in spiritual life. They come to her with their problems, because they heard that Amma is a miracle worker, that she knows everything, that she can give everything, that their problems can be solved just by telling Amma; they have that faith. And certainly, they'll get some relief. But what is Amma's idea in blessing them? By coming to her, they will be put on the path back to God. It is a permanent cure for all problems. Most people come to Amma for a temporary cure. They want to be rid of some sickness, or they want to get a job, or to get married or whatever—all the problems people have. Amma knows that even if one problem is solved, another one is going to crop up. That is the nature of life. Don't be fooled. Even if we solve all our problems, another one will come up and then, finally, the big one comes at the end—death. Amma can't help us there. She can't prevent our body from dying, but she knows that the real cure even for death is God-realization, Self-realization. Darshan helps us towards that final goal.

In the song, *"Ananda Vithi"* written by Amma describing her vision of the Divine Mother and experience of Self-realization, she writes:

> Mother told me to ask the people
> To fulfil their human birth.
> Therefore, I proclaim to the whole world
> The sublime Truth that She uttered,
> "Oh man, merge in your Self!"

This gives us an insight into the divine force motivating Amma's every action, to fulfil the wish of the Divine Mother by showing mankind the way back to their True Self.

Why are Habits so Powerful?

Question: Why are habits so powerful?

Answer: This is obviously a question from a *sadhak*, someone who is doing spiritual practice, because ordinary people don't care much about their habits. They're usually not even aware of them. A sadhak feels choked up by his habits because he is trying to get rid of them and make his mind do what he wants it to do, rather than have to do what the mind makes him do. He wants to become the master of the mind rather than the slave of the mind. Why are habits so powerful? Why do we give in to them so easily? Why do we have such strong resistance to changing our negative habits and making good ones? How does one overcome a negative habit? What if one has tried to do it several times and not succeeded?

Don't think that we have these habits just from this birth alone. They've come from previous births also. Most of the ones we have are from the previous births, and they are called *samskaras*. An individual habit is called a *vasana*. A vasana may also be created in this birth, but the collection that we come with, all the habits that we've developed over the past—our nature—is our *samskara*. That doesn't change with our form. It is a wonder that, even though at death, the *jiva* leaves a body in which it developed all these habits, and then is born into a completely fresh body, it still carries all its habits with it, the same samskaras.

Story of a Mouse that Became a Girl

One day, a mahatma was sitting by the side of a river in deep meditation. Just at that time, a hawk flew by with a tiny female mouse in its claws. As it flew over the mahatma, the mouse struggled and struggled and got out of its claws and fell right onto the lap of the mahatma. He exclaimed, "Oh my, what a poor little creature!" The mahatma had some spiritual powers, so he picked up the mouse and said, "You poor little mouse, I feel so sorry for you. Such a fate shouldn't happen to you again. If I let you go, some other animal may catch you." So he waved his hand over the mouse, and it became a baby girl. He called her Kanti and took her to show his wife. He said, "Dear, you wanted a child for so long, and now here she is," and explained what had happened.

She said, "Okay, I will raise the child as our own daughter."

When the girl became sixteen, they thought, 'We'd better get her married now.' The mahatma said to himself, 'I'll get my daughter married to nobody less than Surya, the sun god.' So he looked at the sun and prayed that the sun god should come down.

The sun god assumed a form and stood in front of him and said, "Swami, what can I do for you? Why did you call me?"

The mahatma called, "Kanti, come here." When Kanti had come, he said to Surya, "I want you to marry my daughter."

When Kanti looked at the sun god, she said, "Daddy, this man is so hot, even stones will melt near him. He'll burn me to ashes. I don't want to marry him, Daddy."

What could he say? "I'm sorry, Surya, but can you suggest somebody else, somebody even more powerful and greater than you?"

Surya said, "Yes, there is somebody."

"Really, who is that?"

"The cloud. The cloud is greater than me, for he can cover my rays. He can prevent me from shining."

So the sage prayed to the cloud, "Please come here." The cloud came flying down and stood there with his big, grey form and deep voice. The mahatma said, "Sir, I'd like you to marry my daughter, Kanti."

Seeing him, Kanti said, "Daddy, he is so loud, and when he talks, he roars like thunder. My eardrums will split every time he speaks. I don't want a husband like that. I want a soft-spoken husband."

"Do you have any suggestions, Mr. Cloud?"

"Yes, the wind is much more powerful than me. He blows me all over the place."

The sage prayed to Vayu, the wind god, who came there and said, "Yes, can I help you?"

"Please marry my daughter, Kanti."

"Daddy, this man wanders all over the place—no steadiness at all! He'll be with me for a moment, and then he'll be off to the other side of the world the next moment. What kind of husband is that? Can't you find somebody that is more suitable?"

"Vayu, can you suggest somebody else?"

"Hmm, there is somebody that I'm unable to blow away."

"Who is that?"

"The mountain, Himavan."

So Himavan was invited to come. When he arrived, he said, "Yes, can I help you?"

"I'd like you to marry my daughter, Kanti. Please, please agree; we have to finish this. Please marry my daughter."

"Daddy, he is so hard-hearted. He is like a stone. I don't want a stone for a husband."

"Do you have any suggestions, Sir?"

"Well, there is somebody more powerful than me."

"Really, who is that?"

"There is a mouse. He is able to dig holes inside me. He can hollow me out completely."

Great! The mahatma invited the mouse.

"Oh, Daddy, he is just what I've always wanted. I've always been looking for such a person to marry. He is so tiny but he is nice, sweet, and perfectly suitable. He is everything I ever wanted in a husband."

"All right," the sage said. "It is true I changed your form, but I couldn't change your samskara, I couldn't change your nature, I forgot about that." So he changed Kanti back into a little mouse, and they lived happily ever after in a hole under the mahatma's hut.

How to Get Rid of Habits?

This is the power of samskara. Even though we change our form, we take the same samskara with us. Then, what is the way to get rid of these deep-rooted habits? First, we've got to understand the nature of habit. Why do we have habits? Everybody's got habits. In fact, that is all we are, consciousness plus habits. If we can get rid of all our habits, then we'll shine as the *Paramatman*, Pure Consciousness. We'll be all *anandam*, bliss. At present, all our energy is diverted through habits. Then, our mind will be perfectly calm, peaceful, blissful.

Where do these habits come from? We want to always be happy. We try to satisfy this desire in the most obvious way, through pleasure of the senses and mind. We are convinced that through pleasure, we will become happy. We engage in actions again and again to experience pleasure and the resulting happiness or peace for a while, but the happiness disappears, leaving the memory behind. This creates a habit. We don't want to be happy only when we are eating or doing other pleasurable things. We want to be happy always. Unknowingly, we might remember, 'I was happy doing such and such a thing. When I watched the TV, it was so much fun.' This thought will not be in so many words, but rather an idea in our subconscious mind. Then we repeat that action again and again. It may even be a mental habit. 'I was happy when I got angry at somebody. I was happy when I was gossiping. I was happy when I was criticizing somebody.' We may remember that pleasant feeling, so we do it again and again. It becomes a habit. It becomes impulsive. A situation arises, and the corresponding habit or impulse springs up. Habits are impulsive actions.

When we're forced to do these things again and again to be happy, life becomes more difficult. That is the next stage—when a habit not only becomes impulsive but compulsive. If we look closely, are we really getting happiness from our habits? Many times, the habits that we've developed get us into a lot of trouble. There are habits like overeating, speeding, and harsh speech. Somebody may lose their job again and again. I heard about someone who was a chronic harsh talker. That must have started at some point. At first, they got their way through harsh speech, and then it became a habit, and then what happened? They started losing their jobs. At home, everybody was miserable. This person was always getting angry, always talking in a mean way. They were miserable because of his making others miserable. Just because of what? Just because of a habit.

Somebody overeats and what happens? They eat themselves to death, or, at the least, they become sick. Someone gets addicted to television, or speeding, or lying, or any destructive habit. There are good habits and there are bad habits. Destructive habits destroy us; they eat away our vitality. They create problems; internally, they make us restless or miserable, and externally, they make everybody unhappy. So we should think, 'Okay, habits are not necessarily good and the pleasure that I'm getting also is not lasting very long. It is like putting a drop of water in a frying pan; the next moment "psst" and it is gone.' When a desire arises, it causes a kind of agitation in the mind and senses which demands satisfaction. On satisfying it and removing that tension, happiness arises, but not for very long, even though we want it to last forever. There is nothing intrinsically wrong with pleasure; it just cannot satisfy our insatiable desire for happiness. Our sense organs cannot be stimulated and satisfied endlessly. At some point, they become jaded. To think that pleasure can be prolonged forever is a misconception. Strangely, everyone has that misconception. The very nature of our mind and senses is that they are limited and changing. We want to be happy forever, but we cannot achieve that either through the changing mind or the senses. Then what is the solution? Are we stuck with this insatiable urge?

We may think: 'What a cruel God to give us such a problem!' Well, we can't question the wisdom of God. Perhaps that mechanism will eventually lead us back to Him. Until then, we have to find a solution. That is where wise people like Amma can help us; where the Vedas, Vedanta and the Ancients (Rishis) have something to say. They tell us that we *can* attain permanent happiness, but not through temporary pleasure. Happiness arises only when our mind becomes still. It comes from within us, from the unmanifest source of our mind. When our mind is concentrated, it becomes still and blissfully peaceful. That is happiness. We want to make that last forever, but we can't through pleasure. Why not try to experience it directly, without depending on the satisfaction born of pleasure as a trigger? If we can make the mind still and one-pointed, then inner stillness will be experienced as our intrinsic nature. When that becomes continuous and full, we will identify with that instead of the restless mind. The source of that stillness is Reality, and we will ultimately merge into That.

How to do it? First understand this: pleasure is temporary and will never satisfy our craving for happiness. We have to reflect on this fact again and again, because we have made this mistake again and again. Pleasure may make us happy for a little while, but that is all. Think about this again and again, not just once in a while. That is the first step.

Next, substitute destructive habits with good habits. We can't just throw away our bad habits. Be happy developing good, constructive habits—doing good things, good actions. Better yet, engage in spiritual actions. For example, try to find happiness in activities like devotional singing, satsang, darshan, reading spiritual books, going on pilgrimage or doing some kind of selfless service.

Mahatmas have told us to practice meditation, mantra *japa* and similar sadhanas. In the beginning, it may be difficult; we won't have any taste for it. However, if we persist and do it regularly, it will become natural and a source of inner peace. Eventually, it will become a good habit and replace the bad habits. Nevertheless, one should be ready for the fight of a lifetime. Purifying the mind is like swimming upstream against the current, trying to reach the source of the river. One needs to go against the flow of Nature to reach the source of the mind.

The *Kathopanishad* says:

> The Self-born has set the doors of the body to face outwards, therefore the soul of a man gazes outwards and not at the Self within: hardly a wise man here and there, desiring immortality, turns his eyes inwards and sees the Self within him.
>
> —*Part 2, ch.1, v.1*

> The good is one thing; the pleasant, another. Both of these, serving different needs, bind a man. It goes well with him who, of the two, takes the good; but he who chooses the pleasant misses the end.
>
> Both the good and the pleasant present themselves to a man. The wise soul examines them well and discriminates. He prefers the good to the pleasant; but the fool chooses the pleasant out of greed.
>
> —*Part 1, ch.2, v.1-2*

> Arise! Awake! Approach the Great and learn. Like the sharp edge of a razor is that path, so the Wise say, hard to tread and difficult to cross.
>
> —*Part 1, ch.3, v.14*

Making a vow will help us to develop will power. Try to stick to a good habit, and if you can't do it or if you fail in this vow, then make yourself do something that you don't like. For example, suppose you are trying to conquer anger but you say an angry word one day. Then, the next day, you should fast as an incentive to not repeat your bad habit. Next time, when you're about to say something in anger, you will think, 'If I say this for the one moment of pleasure that I will get by getting angry, I'm going to have to suffer the whole day tomorrow. I won't be able to eat anything.' Yes, expressing anger is also a kind of pleasure, the pleasure of releasing the pressure built up within. So take a vow like that. That is one way to get rid of a bad habit.

If we can't stop a bad habit abruptly, at least try to reduce its frequency. Maybe we can't stop suddenly. Some people can, some people can't. At least try to reduce it. Suppose today I said something nasty six times; tomorrow I'm going to aim for only five times. It is better not to say anything nasty at all, but at least five is better than six, and the day after tomorrow, four and a half. We can gradually reduce the frequency of our bad habits.

Prayer also helps, invoking a greater power to help us. We should pray to God. "Please rid me of this habit, this weakness." In due course, we will find the habit losing strength.

When we draw a line on a paper with a pencil, erasing it once or twice will be enough to make it disappear. On the other hand, drawing the same line again and again will make it darker and harder to erase. When trying to erase it, there will be some heat caused by the repeated friction. Similarly, it is relatively easy to remove a bad habit when it first begins, but the more we repeat it, the harder it will be to remove. The effort that we make to remove it will result in a kind of uneasiness or heat in our mind. This suffering is called *tapas* (heat) which indicates that the habit is getting erased. It means that we are on the right track towards purification. It is a good sign. The saying "No pain, no gain" applies here. Who made the habit? We made the habit. Who has to break the habit? We have to break the habit. The same energy or more that we put into making it may be needed to get rid of it.

Amma's Advice About Conquering Vasanas

What does Amma say about all this?

"Child, the impressions created by the actions performed in previous births manifest in this birth. These tendencies determine the course of action during this lifetime. What we should do is exhaust them while doing spiritual practice, and avoid adding new ones."

We are born with vasanas in a latent condition. Amma says that we should satisfy our desires, and, at the same time, do sadhana. In that way, our spiritual consciousness will develop and gradually create a feeling of detachment toward the objects of desire. Besides this, we should also not add any new ones.

"Take ten eggs and keep them under a hen to hatch. Suppose one of them is a duck, but the rest are chickens. After being hatched, the duckling takes to water immediately, but what about the chicks? Not a single one will go near the water. That is the nature of vasana. It is derived from the previous birth. Was it not a hen that sat on the eggs? If the vasanas come from the present birth, then the chickens and the duck should act the same.

"The first vasana in a *jiva* (an individual being) is God-given. From that arises karma. From those actions new vasanas arise. All these vasanas accumulate and bring about a new birth. This cycle will continue whirling like a wheel—the wheel of *samsara*, birth, death and rebirth—forever. Liberation from samsara is possible only through attenuation of all the vasanas. Spiritual practices like chanting of the Divine Name, meditation, mantra japa, and satsang all help to weaken the vasanas."

Here is a question asked to Amma a long time ago. Of course, India has changed a lot since then.

Question: "Amma, controlling the mind is not an easy job, especially while living in the midst of worldly pleasures. This is still more difficult for people who live in the West. There, materialism is much stronger than here in India. What advice does Amma have to give concerning this?"

Everybody has desires, everybody has vasanas, but in India, life is simpler. Most people want to get married, have a family, a house, and a good job. Maybe also a bicycle, or if you're wealthy enough, a car. Enjoyments are limited. In the West, however, it is not so simple. People want those things, plus so many other things. They want constantly newer and newer stimuli—more and more complicated, more and more efficient, more and more comfortable. There is an endless flow of wanting something newer, something more pleasant, something more intense; the society is built on that urge. To cater to it, companies make more and more things. There is no limit to it. Maya is very strong there. A simple person who has satisfied his simple desires can think of going beyond to something deeper. However, in a world where pleasure is the goal, there is no end to seeking it, because of so many possibilities. It is more difficult to get any kind of insight into the purpose of life.

In India, a person may go to a general store to get some soap. This will not take much time or cause any distraction. In Western countries, people go to huge malls, which stir up desires that they didn't even know they had. They may spend many hours there, though they came only for a bar of soap!

"Amma is very happy to see the enthusiasm and spirit of the children in the West in wanting to lead a spiritual life. Whoever it may be, vasanas will exist, except in one who has reached the state of Perfection."

Perfection doesn't mean that we become good in something, perfect in something. Perfection means that our mind has become completely silent. It subsides into its source, which is all power and peace. We become perfect in making our mind stop thinking.

"To control the mind means to eliminate the vasanas. Actually, what one should try to do is to remove the previously created vasanas and block the entrance of new ones. This cannot be achieved in a short period of time."

Don't think that we can just decide, 'Okay, I'm going to sit down and my mind is going to keep quiet.' Try it for even half a second. We cannot make our mind stand still for even a moment. That is, unless we've trained our mind to do so over a long period; it is very difficult. Everything we are doing is making it restless, instead of calm.

Amma will not ask us to stop indulging in worldly pleasure completely and devote all our time to spiritual practices. There are people who are interested in doing that, but the majority do not want to, nor can they right away. They want both. They are *bhogis* (one who seeks enjoyment) as well as yogis. We want to lead a worldly life with its pleasures and lead a spiritual life also. For such people, the best way is to slowly and steadily control the vasanas one by one.

"During this process, one might fail many times."

Many devotees say, "I'm trying again and again, but I'm still failing, I still do the same things. I tried a million times and I'm still doing the same things. I'm not making any progress." And then we start to feel sorry about it; we start to feel miserable about it.; we get depressed about it. That is natural. Everybody goes through that stage. Amma says that during this process, one might fail many times.

> "Let failures happen. After all, failure only comes to a person who tries for success. Therefore, do not get worried or agitated if failure happens. It might happen again and again. Nevertheless, do not lose your enthusiasm and interest. Try, again and again."

We know the expression, "If you don't succeed at first, try, try again." That is a very wise saying. Don't waste energy feeling bad about our failures. Just keep trying. In *Srimad Bhagavata,* a yogi asked a sage how he should atone for the bad things he has done. Should he fast, or take a vow of silence, or do some other painful austerities? The sage tells him to keep doing his sadhana, to keep making efforts at self-purification. Austerities may counteract the negative effects of negative actions. They will not, however, purify the mind of its negative tendencies, which are the source of the actions.

> "Declare an open war on your mind. The mind might pull you and push you into the same old habits. Understand that it is only a trick of the great trickster, the mind, to divert you from the path. Do not give up. There will come a point when the vasanas will lose all their strength and give way for the Lord to come in and rule. Till then, try and keep trying. Let the failure fail to stop you from continuing your practice."

Have confidence in Amma's words. If we keep trying to get rid of our vasanas—not just one, but all of them—then at a certain point, they'll become weakened. God's presence will start to shine in us. Amma's presence will start to shine. We'll have an experience, an inner feeling of Amma's presence. That is the real Amma, the real Amma that is in you appearing outside to show you the way to feel her inside. What is obstructing that are only vasanas. It will happen, it has to happen. Spirituality is a science. If we follow the principles, we will get the result. Get rid of the vasanas through sadhana and these techniques, and then we'll feel Amma's presence. Our vasanas will get weaker and weaker and finally disappear.

> "Children, this world is created by the Lord for you to enjoy. No spiritual master or scripture has ever said that anyone should give up all worldly enjoyments and engage in the constant remembrance of God. No one has said that everyone should live in an ashram and become a sannyasin. There are people who can do it and who are determined to do it. Let them follow their path. But there is a way for others also to become closer to God, and that is possible by slowly preparing the mind for that final leap while leading a normal life in this world."

> "While driving, one must obey traffic rules and regulations. If not, accidents will occur. Not only oneself, but others will suffer if an accident happens. Likewise, while driving the vehicle of life along the road of this world, we have to adhere to certain laws, certain dos and don'ts. It is these rules and regulations that the gurus and the scriptures talk about. If we follow them, we can

avoid danger and will be safe both in our personal life and our social life. However, conflicts and calamities will arise in both areas of our life if we break these rules and regulations through over-indulgence and other undisciplined ways."

Amma is saying to have a good time, but be moderate. Don't just do whatever we like. Learn the rules and follow them.

Who is Amma, Really?

Question: If Amma is the Supreme Principle, what does it mean when she says that she is our Guru, birth after birth? Is there an individual soul that has it is own identity that can come and guide us, or is this just a way of saying that Brahman is always guiding us?

Answer: Good question. Brahman is the non-dual Reality, the Infinite Ocean of Consciousness. But the scriptures say that Brahman manifests *Shakti*. There is a vibration in that waveless Ocean of Awareness that is called Shakti, energy. All energy comes out of that stillness and becomes the Creator, Preserver and Destroyer of Creation—Brahma, Vishnu and Shiva. They are the Universal Being in three forms. They can also take a form in this world of matter and in the subtler worlds also. There are *avatars* of Vishnu, like Rama, Krishna and so on. There are avatars of Shiva, such as the sage Durvasa, the hunter Kirat and Adi Shankara. There is also a tradition that believes that the great scholar Mandana Mishra, who debated with Adi Shankara, was an avatar of Lord Brahma. And the Divine Mother, Shakti, also has been born into this world many times. They are all the One only. As Amma says, Brahman is the ocean and the different gods are the waves on the ocean. They assume an appearance of individuality; in their consciousness there is only Brahman. For those who feel that their body is their self, they see an avatar as an individual mind and body. What is not possible for God? As Amma says, everything is an avatar. The whole universe, every atom in it is an avatar of the Absolute Brahman, so why can't Brahman take birth as a human being?

When Amma says that she's been here before, that we've been her devotees or her disciples, or that she's been our Guru again and again, this is what she means. We don't know whether she is Devi or Vishnu or some other aspect of Brahman, but she definitely is Brahman who has assumed a seeming individuality for our sake. These matters are really far beyond our understanding. She says that God can take on a human form for the good of the world. This is explained to Arjuna by Lord Krishna, in the *Bhagavad Gita*.

The Blessed Lord said:
"I taught this imperishable yoga to Vivasvat; Vivasvat taught it to Manu; Manu taught it to Ikshvaku.

This, handed down thus in succession, the King sages learnt. This yoga, by long lapse of time, has been lost here, O harasser of foes.

That same ancient yoga has been today taught to thee by Me, seeing that thou art My devotee and friend; for, this is the Supreme Secret."

Arjuna said:
"Later is Thy birth, and prior the birth of Vivasvat; how am I to understand that Thou taughtest this yoga in the beginning?"

—*Bhagavad Gita, IV, 1-4*

It is the same problem when Amma refers to herself as an ancient being or that she was here before. We say, "How is it possible, Amma; you were born in 1953?" Divine beings come into this world through the power of their Maya, Universal Illusion. This illusion makes us feel that this person is just like ourself, but with some differences.

The Blessed Lord said:

"Many births of Mine have passed, as well as of thine, O Arjuna; all these I know, thou knowest not, O harasser of foes.

Though I am unborn, of imperishable nature, and though I am the Lord of all beings, yet ruling over My own nature, I am born by My own Maya.

Whenever there is a decay of dharma, O Bharata, and an ascendancy of adharma, then I manifest Myself.
For the protection of the good, for the destruction of evil-doers, for the firm establishment of dharma, I am born in every age.

Whoso knows thus My divine birth and action in truth is not born again on leaving this body; he comes to Me, O Arjuna."

—*Bhagavad Gita, IV, 5-9*

One who not just understands, but knows and perceives through experience, that someone is an avatar, Neal Stephen Rosner will merge into God at the end of their life and never have to come back to this world.

Who was Krishna in His previous birth? Traditionally, it is said that He was born as Lord Rama. And before that? The scriptures (like the *Bhagavatam*) about Lord Vishnu say that He has come as many avatars. Who can say who Amma was before? When asked, she said that if we want to compare her to someone of the past, compare her to Lord Krishna!

What is the Meaning of Life?

Question: How can the lives of these countless beings be meaningless? Isn't life God's manifestation?

Answer: Who says that they are meaningless? The purpose of life and the purpose of individuality is very clear and it is supremely important. It is to return to one's source, which is Eternal Bliss. Everybody always wants unending happiness. The attainment of that is the purpose of life. The pleasures that we experience in life exhaust our desires. The pains that we experience in life increase our detachment, our surrender, our devotion, our seriousness, our patience, our wisdom. Ultimately, through the path of pleasure and pain, we will make the effort to bring us back to the starting point, to square one, our own Real Self. As Amma and the scriptures say, we are already one with the Absolute. It is not that we've got to go somewhere and become one with God. God is already there in us. God has become us. That sense of existence and consciousness, the 'I' that shines within our mind, is God. Unfortunately, our attention is not on that but on other things.

Vasanas are the habits that draw our mind or attention away from the 'I', away from the core of our being. If we can be rid of all these habits so that the mind becomes still, with no movement at all, then this illusion of individuality, the feeling that the body is our self, will dissolve into the One, and we will realize our oneness with that. It is not that something has to rain down from heaven on us. Only our mind has to become completely still. That is the gospel of Vedanta. That is Amma's experience, and that is what we're aiming for—to make the mind perfectly still. Life is not insignificant. The purpose of life is to take us back to the Source, to the Self.

What is the Purpose of the Different Sadhanas?

Question: What is the difference between the results of chanting and the results of meditation? Is there any harm in doing only one of these activities but not the other?

Answer: The purpose of any sadhana, be it a devotional sadhana like bhajan, or *puja*, or meditation and self-enquiry, is to gain concentration of mind on something that represents Reality for us, and then ultimately to experience Reality, to gain the perception of Reality. The condition that is necessary to experience the Atman or the Self is a concentrated, one-pointed, calm mind. When we do bhajan, our heart gets calm and our mind gets concentrated in the heart. When we do meditation, our mind gets sharpened. It gets quiet and our concentration gets one-pointed. We may notice that when we feel more devotion, we also get more concentration, more one-pointedness. Also, when we have good one-pointedness, devotion will increase; so bhajan leads to meditation and meditation leads to bhajan. It is not that we've got to do one or the other. They are interrelated—you can't separate them. Some people are more devotional-minded, and some people are more intellectual, more inclined towards the path of *jñana* or knowledge. Either one can be done fully, or mixed; it doesn't matter, because all roads lead to Rome. And both of them increase each other. One's mood and strength of mind may vary, and so also may the type of sadhana.

Where Do We Go After Death?

Question: If someone does many evil acts and is sentenced to death, does their removal from this life mean that evil is reduced on the planet? If so, are we increasing the evil on the other side by putting murderers to death?

Answer: This is a very strange question. Removing evildoers definitely reduces the evil in the world; there is no doubt about it. As Lord Krishna says and as we just read,

> "For the protection of the good, for the destruction of the evildoers, for the establishment of dharma, I'm born in every age."

Why does God come to this plane of existence? One of the reasons is to destroy the evildoers. According to the scriptures of India, like the *Srimad Bhagavatam*, the Earth, Bhudevi, is a living being. What we see as the earth is the physical body of a goddess. When there are too many evildoers, she feels it as a burden and wants to be rid of it, so she prays to God saying, "Please remove my burden." That is when an Avatar descends. When things are getting too bad, when the balance of Nature is very disturbed, He comes.

As far as increasing the evil on the other side, we don't have to worry about that. There is a special world for the evildoers after they leave their body. They have their own place, called *Narakaloka*, hell. There are twenty-seven separate hells. It is a very big place. They have no freedom there to do evil. It is a life of non-stop suffering and punishment.

There is also Heaven. That is where one has only a good time. Some people don't want to have just a pleasant time. They are spiritual-minded devotees. They go to Vaikunta or Mt. Kailasa, Shivaloka or Goloka, or they may want to go to the heavens where Jesus or Mohammed are. There are many different heavenly worlds. There they have a devotional lifestyle, just like we have here; we enjoy bhajans, darshan, etc. When we go to the other worlds, we stay there until the karma that took us there gets exhausted, and then we come back to this world. We go back and forth, back and forth, until we get tired and fed up with it, and finally make the effort to sink within to our Self, the inner light of the Atman or Supreme Bliss, and wake up from this long dream. That is the end of the story.

Amma's Way of Moulding Us

Question: I have found that, by praying to Amma, I can get my desires fulfilled and overcome various kinds of misfortunes. However, praying for these things creates a distraction and takes away any bliss I may feel when I am close to her. Does this mean that one should not pray for help and let calamities befall us if such is our prarabdha? If many calamities befall us, should we just continue with our sadhana and take it as Amma's will?

Answer: We may be having some actual suffering, be it physical or mental or circumstantial, so we come to Amma for relief. She wants to help us evolve towards the experience of our oneness with God. She looks upon us like the sculptor looks at a stone. She sees that divine potential in us.

There is a story about Michaelangelo. One day, he was walking down the street where there was some construction work going on. A lot of granite and marble stones were strewn about in the yard. They were the leftovers from the construction and were going to be thrown away.

He said to the workers, "I want one of the stones. I will even pay for it."

The workers asked, "What do you want a useless stone for?"

He replied, "You see it as a useless stone, but I see an angel in it. All it needs is a little work. Put it in my front yard, and I'll make it into an angel." A sculptor sees the potential in a stone.

Similarly, Amma sees us as the Paramatman, as Brahman, as God. She knows that we need just a little work. She asks us to park ourselves in her front yard so that she can work on us. However, we don't want to sit quietly in the yard; we feel restless. Amma showers love and affection on us and shows us that she knows everything. She shows us that she sees our heart. She binds us with her love so we don't wander away.

One day, she takes up the hammer and chisel and lightly chips here and there so that our shape starts to change. It may hurt a little sometimes, but then Amma gives us a pat and a kiss and we feel okay. She says, "Don't worry, I am with you always," and shows us that she really is. Then she starts to chisel an outline. Still, she keeps showing love and affection and understanding. We continue coming to Amma, thinking that she will remove all our problems and make us happy. Amma knows that removing the problems is not the cure. A minor fix is not enough; we need a complete overhaul. So she removes some of our suffering, but also she leaves some so that we should struggle and thereby become strong. A person who wants to develop their muscles needs heavy weights to work out with. In the same way, she leaves some of the difficulties for us to struggle with. Otherwise, how are we going to get strong? How are we going to develop detachment and patience? How are we going to get all the good qualities that we need to evolve? They won't come just by themselves; some circumstances have to bring them about.

An occasional scolding or correction may be there. Because of our experience of Amma's love for us, our faith increases. We come to understand that Amma is really doing something to us; not just a superficial dusting but a deep cleaning. Our life is changing, our personality is getting purified. We are getting some devotion, some concentration. Yet at the same time, other problems are persisting. The difficulties are persisting. Maybe they're even getting worse. Nevertheless, while Amma goes on chipping away, our shape is slowing changing. And after we finally get into a recognizable shape, we begin to feel Amma's presence inside us. We start to realize that which is outside as Amma is inside as her presence, as the presence of God.

Then there is no question of ever leaving Amma; she is always there. There is no question of praying to Amma for favours because she is always shining in us and everything is being taken care of, even unto death and beyond. After all, suppose Amma removes all our problems and everything is rosy. Then what? Is our body going to live forever? No. Finally, death will come. What are we going to do at that time? Even now, we should be doing that—surrendering to God. Through surrender, divine light starts to increase more and more, the darkness of individuality and ignorance gets less and less, and then, finally, there is nothing left except Amma. Any difficulty is seen as a mere dream. That is what yoga is all about—the end of suffering, the attainment of bliss. That is what Amma does to us when we come to her. She wakes us up fully so we realize that individuality is an illusion. Is there a wave separate from the sea?

Are Dreams a Reliable Source of Guidance?

Question: Can we be guided by what Amma says in dreams? If we pray for guidance and someone suggests a solution for a problem, can we assume that it comes from Amma?

Answer: Dreams may or may not be a reliable source of guidance or inspiration. The same applies to people. We may have a problem and pray to God for help. Later, someone may give us advice and we may get into trouble by following it. Neither depending on others as instruments of God nor interpreting dreams as coming from God and Guru are completely foolproof. We've got to discriminate. Also, we shouldn't be gullible. Thinking that anything anybody says is guidance coming from God can definitely get us into trouble.

When I first arrived in India, I thought every person that had a beard must be a holy man! Going for a walk outside the Calcutta airport, I saw a taxi driver who had a long beard standing by his car. I jumped. 'Wow! A real saint, a mahatma, I finally saw a mahatma!' I thought. I told my brother, "Look at his eyes, they're so full of divine light. He must be a mahatma." Much later, I realized that he probably wasn't a mahatma but just a bearded man like millions of other men in India. I was very gullible.

"Credulity in the man is weakness, but in the child is strength."
—*Charles Lamb, 18th Century*

It is good to be innocent, but it is not good to be a fool.

Sometimes it is true that we have some dreams that give us some insight and some guidance, but we can't trust all of them. We can accept the seemingly good ones, follow them a bit, and see if there is any use in that, or, otherwise drop it. Don't become a devotee of your dreams, and don't believe everything that everybody says to you or follow all the advice that everybody tells you. Suppose you're sick. You know what usually happens? If you live in a community of fifteen people and you've got a bad cough, you'll get fifteen different treatments, and you'll become half dead from trying all of them. It happens like that; everybody has got their cure and their opinion. We have to be careful, we have to discriminate.

Accept Life and Death as Amma's Grace

Question: As devotees living in this seismically active state of California, what is Amma's advice to safeguard ourselves and our families? Is San Francisco going to plunge into the Pacific Ocean?

Answer: Some of you might have been wondering why I was talking to Dr. Iyer, who works at the U.S. Geological Survey, just before I came here. I wanted to get the advice of our very own in-house earthquake specialist. Unfortunately, Dr. Iyer cannot stop earthquakes, but he can tell us what is going to happen, only not when. He said that California will not fall into the ocean. At the most, the land will shift for about a hundred miles, but not go into the ocean. It'll move north and south, since that is the way the fault line runs. It may shift a lot, even twelve meters or thirty or forty or even fifty feet, but it is not just going to crack off and fall into the ocean with us on it. That won't happen. Maybe in the course of tens of millions of years, slowly it may gradually go into the ocean, but not suddenly one day. It is not going to happen like that.

That is from the standpoint of science. Nobody knows exactly when an earthquake is going to happen, but everybody knows that there is going to be a big earthquake in this area. So what is Amma's advice? There is no special advice. We've got to continue doing what we're doing. We cannot be worrying about what is going to happen every moment; otherwise, what will we be? We'll be a bundle of worries all the time. We won't be able to live. Anyhow, our fate is already decided. Before we were born, it was decided how we are going to leave the body. We can't do anything about it, so why worry about it?

There is a story about a man who heard that, according to his horoscope, he was going to be eaten by an alligator, so he never went near water. Yet somehow, when he got very old, his grandson fell into a river and, without thinking, he jumped in to save the child. Just then, an alligator came and ate him. It was his fate. He was so careful, yet it happened. Similarly, if it is our destiny to be in an earthquake, so be it. We can't alter that. We need not bother about it; we need not fear that. We need not even fear death. We should always be aware that at any moment, death might come due to some cause or other. Our heart may stop; we don't need an earthquake. The body is such a delicate little thing; anything can make it stop. The heart stops, or we're in a car accident; somebody shoots us. Anything can happen. There are so many ways to die, no shortage.

King Yudhisthira said in the *Mahabharata* that the greatest wonder in the world is that everybody thinks that everyone else will die, but not himself. It is a delusion to think like that, but there is some truth to it. Why do we think that we're never going to die? Everybody feels like that. The fact is that the eternally existing *jiva* (soul) residing temporarily in a body, will not die, but the body definitely will. Amma says that we will be the witness of the death of the body, yet we will remain as the soul, as the Atman. Whatever is born dies, and whatever is not born doesn't die. The body came into existence. We're connected to it, we're attached to it, it is going to leave us and we'll be the same as we were before we were born. We just don't remember, that is all. We have a short memory. We can't even remember what happened yesterday, what to say of at the time of birth or before that? It doesn't mean that we didn't exist.

We've taken refuge in a Satguru, in Amma, a person who is one with Brahman. She says that anyone who makes that connection is looked after for eternity. That is the connection that we have to make, just one time. Take refuge in Amma. Then, for all eternity, for all our future births until we merge into our Self, Amma will be looking after us. We don't have to pray again and again, "O Amma, please save me. Did you hear me last time? Just in case you didn't hear me last time, I'm asking you this time again. Shall I say it louder? I cried only five minutes last time, I'll cry ten minutes this time." We don't have to do that. One time, just turn to Amma in our heart, and one time say, "Amma, please save me, I take refuge in you." She'll save us. No doubt. She has given that assurance.

In the *Ramayana*, when Vibhishana, the brother of Lord Rama's enemy, Ravana, took refuge in Rama, the Lord said, "This is My promise, that anybody who takes refuge in Me even once, is Mine from then onward." So we need not concern ourselves about our life and death, the sufferings that we're going to have to go through. It is all Amma's *prasad*. We should accept it as such. The painful things are prasad, and the pleasant things also are prasad. Krishna liberated a whole group of kings. They were suffering; they were going to be offered in a human sacrifice. He liberated them and said to them, "Henceforth, consider everything that happens to you in the future as My prasad. Your death is My prasad, your sufferings are My prasad, your rebirth is My prasad, your pleasures are My prasad. Everything is My prasad. That is what you should think. Do your sadhana and consider your life as My prasad, My gift." So try to hold onto that thought even if the place is shaking or whatever may happen, accept it all as Amma's prasad.

Questions and Answers - 1

Better Reach the Inner Silence than Talk to Others

Question: Recently, I was relating an experience I had during meditation to a fellow devotee. I was admonished for discussing it, and was told that experiences should never be revealed to anyone. Does discussing spiritual experiences dispel the positive energy?

Answer: Before one tells one's experiences, one should weigh one's motives very carefully. Not only that. Before everything that we say, everything that we do, we should think as to why we are saying or doing it. When it comes down to something like spiritual experience, why are we telling somebody our experience? Is it to inspire them? Do they want to be inspired by us? Or is it to impress people, that they should think something great about us? We have to see. If it is to inspire others, we should make sure that we're a person who can inspire others or that people want to be inspired by us. And if it is just out of ego, we should be careful. We shouldn't do that, because in spiritual life, the more the ego is fed, the further away we're getting from God. It is the ego that is hiding the sun from shining in our heart, the sun of God.

There was a disciple who always wanted to impress others with his spiritual experiences. In front of the Guru, and making sure that others were around to hear it, he would say, "O Guru, I had a great meditation and was so blissful at that time." Real gurus are not fooled. Even if we don't know what our motives are, the Guru knows. So he thought, 'Just telling this fellow is not going to do any good. I'll have to send him away from here and let him do sadhana somewhere else. Then only he'll stop dissipating his energy and feeding his ego like this.' So he was sent away to a holy place, Brindavan. The Guru said, "Write to me every six months about your spiritual progress."

Now he was alone. Solitude is a good way to do sadhana if we have a guru. If we don't have a guru, it is better not to do that. We may not be aware of all the dirt that is in our mind. In any case, we should have a guru.

After six months, he wrote a letter, "Dear Guruji, *pranams*. My meditation is going very well. I'm meditating so many hours every day and getting good concentration. I'm seeing divine lights and divine forms." Six months later another letter comes, "Oh, Guruji, I'm really flying high. I'm seeing everything as God; there is divine light around everything and I'm so blissful." Then after another six months, "Dear Guruji, I'm having good meditation." Not much of a letter. Another six months (now two years have passed), "Dear Guruji, pranams." That was the letter. Then after six months, there was no letter. And after one year, still no letter. Then after one and a half years, the Guru sent somebody to get him. They brought him back, and he just did his namaskaram and sat quiet in a corner.

The Guru said, "Come on, tell us. We've been waiting all these days. What is happening? How is your meditation?" The disciple didn't say anything. "Tell us, come on. You always used to be so restless. You wanted to tell us about how good you were meditating and all your experiences."

"What is there to tell, Guruji? My mind has become so still that I can't think anymore. No thoughts come; nothing comes out of my mouth. With great effort I am saying this. And I realize also that I don't even exist. Only you exist, so I can't even say pranams. There is no me anymore, there is only you."

That is the state that we have to reach. That is what Amma says, that the mind has to become so still that you don't feel like talking. You don't feel like saying anything. You don't even think; it is just bliss—quiet, peaceful bliss. You live in the world of perfect bliss. There is no urge to talk. You don't care about anything except drinking from the inner spring of bliss. So, if we haven't reached that stage, it is probably better not to discuss our experiences with others.

Questions & Answers - 2 & Divine Qualities

(Questions put to Swami during Satsang time)

Sri Krishna talks about the qualities found in a person born for the 'divine lot' in the 16th chapter of the *Bhagavad Gita*. The first quality is fearlessness. Why fearlessness? Because the sages say that the mind's two basic *vasanas* are desire and fear. Because of them, the mind remains in an agitated state much of the time. In that state, it is impossible to perceive one's True Nature as the Atma.

Purity of Heart

The next quality is purity of heart. Purity of heart means having only *sattvic* thoughts and feelings. Christ also said,

> "Blessed are the pure in heart, for they shall see God."
>
> —New Testament, Matthew 5.8

Doing sadhana helps to purify the mind. Sadhana means bhajan, japa, meditation, satsang and so on. That alone is not sufficient for the awakening of spiritual consciousness. We also have to consciously cultivate divine qualities so that their opposites do not find a place in us.

Amma uses the example of ants and sugar. If we collect sugar and then let ants eat it, what happens? There will be nothing left after sometime. Collecting sugar is like doing sadhana, and, at the same time, allowing negative tendencies to persist, is like letting the ants eat it.

Many people come to Amma and say, "I have been doing sadhana for a long time. I have been meditating for twenty five or thirty years. I spent that time with this saint and that guru, but still have no spiritual experience."

The answer is always the same. "You were doing sadhana, it is true; but the fruits of your sadhana were leaking out in many places."

Anger, fear, worry, hatred, envy—all these negative vasanas consume the energy that we accumulate through the self-control generated by sadhana. Why should we try to save energy? Because, if we save it, we gain the inner strength of mind to make the waves of negative thoughts and feelings reduce. Then we start to feel peace within our mind; we start to experience our real Self. Our sense of divinity, our *swarupa* or real nature will start to manifest. It is as simple and logical as that. The Truth is within us as the source of our life and mind. It is veiled by tamasic and rajasic thoughts and feelings. These are like muddy water that prevents us from seeing the river bed. We need to lead our life in the right way (dharma) so that the mind will calm down.

Become Innocent Like a Child

Purity of heart implies absence of deceit, not telling lies, not being crooked or fault-finding; in other words, to be innocent like a child. Just think of what an innocent child is like. Of course, not all children are innocent, as we all must have noticed. Some are more innocent than others; some have very little innocence. Just imagine the most innocent child that we have ever seen, and then try to be like that. We don't want to be child*ish*. We want to be mature and wise, but at the same time, childlike.

Why does everybody feel so attracted to an innocent child? Whoever we are, we may be the greatest mahatma or an ordinary person—when we see an innocent child, there is a kind of simple happiness we feel in our heart. We want to go nearby and watch them for sometime. That is divinity. That is God. If we look at Amma, she frequently expresses that same innocent nature, yet she is completely mature and wise in her divinity. The innocent soul is most dear to God and Guru. He may have no other redeeming quality, but that is preferable than being clever and proud. Such a person is extremely rare. When Adi Sankaracharya posed the question: who is a scholar envious of? His answer was: the naturally humble person.

Story of the Innocent Janitor

There is an interesting story about a very innocent person who received God's protection. This happened a long time ago. There once lived a king who was surrounded by crooked ministers. One day, they told him, "There is a certain religious community in the town who are troublemakers. We should ask them to leave the kingdom." These ministers were jealous of these people's wealth and wanted to get rid of them, so they convinced the king to banish them.

When this community heard about it, they went to the king and said, "What is this? We didn't do anything wrong. Why are you going to ask us to leave? Are we just supposed to pick up all our generations worth of life and businesses and culture and go? This is unfair!"

The king said, "All right, we'll make a deal. We'll have a debate. If you win the debate, you can stay. The debate will be in pantomime, which means sign language. No words—a silent debate."

The people went back home and gathered all the religious leaders together in their temple. Who is going to represent the people to the king? Nobody was willing. It was too much of a responsibility. If they lose the debate, the whole community is going to be kicked out of the town. So everyone was afraid, and nobody would do it. Meanwhile, the janitor of the temple, the man who cleans the place, was listening.

He said, "What is the difficulty? I'll do it!"

"You will do it? You don't know anything! You only know how to hold a broomstick!"

"None of you are willing to do it, so let me try."

"All right, do it. There is no one else."

The next day, the king and the sweeper met. The king went first. He pointed his finger at the horizon. The janitor pointed his finger at the ground.

Then the king held his finger up to the janitor's face. The janitor took three fingers and held them up to the king.

Then the king took out an apple from his pocket and held it. The janitor had a paper bag with him. He opened it up, took out a piece of bread and held it.

The king said, "You win. You can stay here!" He went back inside his room where all the advisors were.

They said, "What happened, Maharaj?"

The king said, "There was no way that I could have defeated that man. He is brilliant; he is a genius. Such a philosopher doesn't exist in this country."

"What do you mean, Maharaj, what happened?" they exclaimed.

"Well, I went like this (pointing at the horizon), and I meant that the whole world is ruled over by God. And then he went like this (pointing to the ground), and what he was saying was, 'It is true, the whole world is ruled by God, but there is a place called hell, and in hell somebody else is in charge. There is the devil.'

Then I went like this (pointing a finger in his face) to say, 'God is One.' Then he went like this (pointing three fingers in the king's face) to say, 'God is One, but He manifests as the Creator, the Preserver, the Destroyer.' Then I thought, 'What am I to do with this man? I better change the subject.' So I took out the apple and showed it to him. I was referring to the latest theory that the world is round. Then he took out a piece of bread to show me that the scriptures and tradition say the earth is flat. Then I thought, 'Even in science I can't defeat this man,' so I gave up. Let them stay."

Meantime, the other party were going berserk! They were carrying the janitor on their shoulders through the streets and there was such an uproar! Finally, they brought him to the temple and asked him what happened. "Congratulations! What happened, how did you defeat him?"

"Defeat him? Oh, it was a bunch of nonsense."

"What do you mean, a bunch of nonsense?"

"First, the king pointed to the horizon. He was saying, 'All of you have to get out of this country.' Then I pointed to the ground, meaning 'No, we are going to stay here!' Then he stuck his finger in my face. He meant, 'You arrogant fellow!' So I stuck up three fingers, to say, 'You are three times as arrogant!' Then he took out his lunch, so I took out mine also!"

Can you remember when you were a child? I remember. I didn't come from a family that was religious. The people in my house weren't concerned with that subject. They would only go to the temple on holy days as a matter of social etiquette. Despite that, I remember looking up in the sky and imagining that the clouds were God; He had a big white beard and long white hair, and was looking down on everybody.

I had a cousin who was also my closest friend, and we used to play all the time. When I was very young, maybe seven years old, we used to play with paper airplanes. We would fold up a piece of paper and throw it. Well, paper airplanes don't fly very well. My cousin was about fifty feet away from me and holding up his hand, said, "If you can hit my hand with that airplane, I will give you all the money that I have in my pocket,"—which was about ten cents! I closed my eyes and prayed for the impossible. 'O God, please God, let me hit his hand with the airplane. I want that ten cents more than anything.' I wasn't very ambitious. I threw the plane and it went all over the place, and finally hit his hand! Ahhh! I was in ecstasy. I felt God truly exists and He is looking after me. He heard my prayers. I was sure there was a God. It was natural to feel so at that young age.

Once, I heard that another friend of mine was moving away because his parents got another job somewhere else. That night I prayed, 'O God, don't let them move away.' The next day, my friend told me, "My father lost his new job. We are not moving away after all. We're going to stay here." These small incidents gave me an innocent faith in God. When I got older, when the world became a concrete reality, that relationship with God disappeared. That is what happens if our family is not devotional. It was only after I came to India that I started to believe in God again. It is natural to believe in God in India.

Once, a child took some cookies that his mother had kept aside after cooking them. She wanted to give them to the other family members when they came home from work and school. Noticing this, his mother said to him, "Did you know that when you stole those cookies from the kitchen, God was there?"

The child said, "Yes, Mommy."

"And did you know that He was looking at you the whole time?"

"Yes, Mommy."

"And what do you think He was saying to you?"

The child said, "He was saying, 'There is nobody here except the two of us, so why don't you take one for Me also!'"

Steadfastness in Knowledge and Yoga

The next quality is steadfastness in knowledge and yoga. What kind of knowledge? Knowledge here means *jñana*. Jñana means Self-knowledge, to experience our real Self, our True Nature. Yoga means to merge in that knowledge; the mind should unite with That.

> "Yoga is the suppression of the modifications of the mind. Then the Seer abides in Itself."
>
> —*Yoga Sutras, Bk.1, v.2-3*

For that to happen, we first need to gain a clear intellectual understanding of the goal through study of the Vedanta philosophy. Vedanta says that we have a body and a mind, but we are not the body or the mind; they are our possessions. Although we are connected to them through the nervous system, we are distinct from them.

If we still the restless mind, the experience of our Real Self can dawn. Vedanta teaches us to be quiet, to still the mind. When the sun is setting, nature becomes quiet. The birds stop chirping and many animals cease their activities and become still; everything in nature becomes quiet except our mind. The outer nature may become quiet, but the inner nature—the mind—goes on thinking as usual.

The object of spiritual practice is to quieten the mind so that the Self can be experienced. The mind is like a lake and the waves on the lake are like the thoughts in the mind. The moon in the sky is like the Self that can be seen on the surface of the mind only if the waves subside. But in this case, the Self is within us, and the thoughts obstruct its perception.

Many people don't believe that being born, living, and then dying is all there is to existence. There must be something more. Numerous people who have had darshan of Amma have come away with a deep experience of peace and bliss that they never even knew existed. Amma awakens a desire in them to gain that peace through spiritual practice or sadhana. She tells them that they must find that within themselves, that God who is bliss and peace is there as the source of their own mind. One does not have go to far away galaxies to find Him. That Being is the core of our mind.

Find God Within Yourself First

Once, a prince came to a mahatma and said, "Swamiji, I want to see God, I want to meet God. I heard that God is the greatest." The swami said, "I'll introduce you to Him, but first you have to tell me who you are?"

"Swamiji, what is the problem? I am the prince of the local village."

"That is not who you are. That is just who your body is. Are you the body?"

"Yes, I am the body."

"How can you be the body?" The swami caught hold of the prince's nose and squeezed it, "Are you the nose?" He caught hold of his ear and twisted it, "Are you the ear? If you are the body, then you are the ear and nose also."

"Oh," the prince said, "I am wrong, Swamiji. Those are mine. It is my nose; it is my ear. Please stop squeezing."

"Right. They are yours; they are not you. Then who are you?"

"I must be the mind."

"How can you be the mind? Sometimes your mind is restless; sometimes it is peaceful, sometimes it is happy, sometimes it is sad, sometimes it is dull, sometimes it is sharp. Sometimes you say 'my mind'; many times a day you say it."

"Ah, you're right, Swamiji. I'm something else. The mind also belongs to me; it is not me."

"Then who are you? First tell me who you are. Then I'll introduce you to God."

The prince sat there with his eyes closed. He said, "I don't know who I am, Swamij. You've got me there."

That is a problem for spirituality and Vedanta; you can understand it up to that point and then you can't go beyond that point with your mind. Only sadhana, only *tapas* will get you beyond there.

Swamiji said, "Listen. Let me ask you a question. What have you done today before you came here?"

The prince said, "Well, I got up in the morning. I went to the bathroom. I had my shower. I had a cup of coffee. I read the newspaper, and now I came here."

"That is all? You only did five or six things?"

"That is all Swamiji. After all, how much can a person do in the morning?"

"No, you have done thousands of things this morning, thousands of things."

"I don't remember anything; this is all I did. I'm not that busy."

"Didn't you digest your breakfast? Didn't you grow your hair? Aren't your lungs breathing in and out? Aren't you sweating? What about your circulation? Didn't you do all those things?"

"Swamiji, I didn't do all those things. They just happened."

"They just happened? If you left your body, if you died, would they continue to happen? No! So you're doing them. You may not be doing them voluntarily; involuntarily, you're doing all those things. So what is it that is doing all those things? That is you!"

"Swamiji, it is becoming clear. There is something, some presence that is making everything work—the body, the mind and all the involuntary actions. That is the 'me'. But still it is not quite clear. Can you say a little more please?"

"Sure. When you're awake, you're conscious of this body, you identify with this body. You're aware of this body in this world. And then, when you go to sleep, this body and this world aren't there anymore. What is there? Then there is another world, a dream world, and you have a different body in the dream world. You're aware of that body in that world, and then when you don't dream and you're also not awake, where are you? Then you're in deep sleep, no dreams, dreamless sleep. Mind is shut off. There is no sense perception, but you are aware. There is an awareness in sleep also. In fact, we like it so much that, if we don't get that sleep every night, we're miserable. Can you imagine dreaming all night long, every night? That would be terrible; nobody would want to go to sleep. When we are deep sleep, we're still aware, a dim awareness, but of what? Darkness, peace, rest, bliss. The awareness that is there, the awareness that is in dreams, and the awareness that is now in the waking state—it is the same, isn't it?"

The prince said, "Ah, Swamiji, now I understand. That is who I am; I'm awareness."

"Yes."

"Alright, Swamiji, now what about God? You said you would introduce me to God as soon as I told you who I am. I'm awareness. Who is God, what is God?"

Then the swami said, "Look at the trees, look at the grass. Look at all the things that are growing. Do you think that the force that makes them grow is different than the force that makes the hair on your body grow?"

"No, it must be the same thing."

"So, what makes the hair on the body grow?"

"Me."

"Then what makes the things on the earth grow?"

"The same thing, me—awareness."

"Then I just introduced you to God, your own Self. That is what God is. That thing that is you, your real Self, is also the Self of everything, and that is God. By knowing your Self, you will know God."

Once we understand that, then we should gradually fill ourself with that idea, that 'I am awareness'. Meditate on it, try to get the experience of it, get a glimpse of that. It will come. If we are doing sadhana properly, we will get this experience of ourself as awareness, as a kind of subtle current of light, different than the physical body.

If we are on the devotional path, meditating on the formless God, we'll feel the presence of God, the dearest of the dear. If we are meditating on a form of God, we may see God and feel God's Presence radiating from that form.

Experiencing the Reality in our mind must come, but we must exert to get that experience; it is not cheap. It is like nothing in this world, it is so unique, so blissful. We may get anything in this world, but it will only make us happy for some time. It is not like that with the experience of the Self. If you get it, it is so interesting, pleasurable and enjoyable, and the more you get, the more you want. You never get tired of it, you never get bored with it. Some people say, "Who wants God? How boring! He is just nothing, like space. What can you do with space? I want something fun. I want something interesting."

God is the most interesting thing there is. Your own Self is the most interesting. If you can contact that, a fountain of bliss will come out, and you'll never get tired of that, you'll always be aware of that and become full of that. Then you wwill see everything as full of that. When you put green sunglasses on, everything becomes green. When your mind becomes full of the Divine Presence, then you see everything as covered with Divinity, like an ocean—the Ananda Sagara, the Ocean of Bliss. It is not beyond us; that is what we are here for. That is what we're born for, to experience that, not just to live as ordinary human beings.

That is what Amma is teaching. That is what radiates from Amma. That is why we like to be with Amma so much. We can never be with Amma enough. Why? It is because of that presence, that bliss which is radiating from her; but we can get it from within ourself also. In fact, we have to. That is the ultimate purpose of being with Amma—to awaken what is already inside us. It is like a fire lighting a fire. That must become perfectly natural. Now we naturally feel that we're a body. When we feel, "I am that presence, I am that vast awareness," that is called yoga, being established in the state of being the Atman. Yoga is the experience of being That.

Expand the Heart Through Charity

The next quality is charity. What does charity have to do with Self-realization? Some people think, 'If I give a lot of money to a temple or church, God will give me Self-realization.' That is not God if He does like that! Then how did all the poor saints become God-realized souls? It must not have been by giving their money; they had no money to give. There are so many sannyasis that have nothing, and they became *jñanis*, Self-realized people.

So why charity? What do we need charity for? Generally, human beings are very attached to the things of the world, especially money and possessions, and that attachment is for a good reason. It could be for survival or for enjoyment, pleasure, or comfort. Whatever the reason is, it creates an attachment and a very concrete sense of reality to this world.

Vedanta and Amma say that this world is like a dream; we are here now, but we may be gone the next minute. As Shakespeare said,

> "All the world's a stage,
> And all the men and women merely players;
> They have their exits and their entrances,
> And one man in his time plays many parts."

Don't think that this is our home; don't think we are going to live here forever. We came here a little while ago and we will be leaving soon. We are on the stage for a few minutes, and then we have to leave. That is all. If we can feel that it is a dream, then we can experience the Self, the Atma. If the world feels real and concrete, then the Atma seems like a dream. Unfortunately, we don't even have the sense of the Atma or God. The more concrete and real the world is, the more abstract and unreal God or the Self is.

So how do we get rid of the feeling that this is so concrete? Children are like that. They don't feel a sense of reality in this world. Remember when we were kids? The world was like a dream and then slowly it solidified. As we got older, the dreaminess reduced and became hard, stiff; it became a reality. We can be happy, even now, if we feel this world is a dream. Even suffering and death become part of the dream. They are not so serious. We'll always be blissful.

Attachment! That gives this dream a sense of reality and hides the actual Reality. By giving of ourselves, we create a sense of unreality in the world, an expansion of our heart. Amma says that most people in the present age are in their head. Their intellect is expanded and their heart is shrunk.

When somebody says, "Hey you!" we answer, "Who me?" Where are we pointing? Nobody points to their head saying, "Who me?" They point to their heart. Not the physical heart; that is not the heart we're talking about. We're talking about the soul, where we see God, where we experience the Atman. It is in the heart, not in the head. In the head, we may see things, but we feel them in the heart. To feel, the heart has to be developed. For many of us, it is now like an atrophied muscle. It is not being used, so it has become weak and flabby. We've got to use it. If we don't do anything to awaken our heart, it will become an inert blob or it will dry up like a prune. It will shrink, it will close. Then all we will be is a big head. Have you seen ticks when they are biting an animal? There is a huge thing sticking out with a tiny little head. The body is so big. It will be the other way around. We'll be a big head with a little heart.

We've got to be careful. We've got to develop our heart. We've got to make it big, make it broad. That is where charity comes in. The happiness of giving a thing is different than the happiness of enjoying a thing. When we enjoy a thing, our head gets big. When we give a thing, our heart gets big. That makes it closer to God, closer to the Self. However, there is one danger when we give. We've got to be careful of the ego. 'I gave that. I did this for somebody. I gave so much money for that poor fellow. I'm great. I'm a philanthropist. I'm a big giver.' We shouldn't even think like that much less talk like that. We should be doing that for our own self-improvement. To make us improve, we give. Let others be improved by it. Don't think we're helping them. Don't use the word 'help.' We can say 'serve.' I'm serving them. Actually, we're serving ourself; we're not serving anybody else when we give. It helps us. Never mind about the other person. Give for our own self. Everyone loves themself the most anyhow, so give for our own self. From the viewpoint of karma, whatever we give is anyhow going to come back to us. Even otherwise, this will help us expand our heart.

If we're proud about it, the positive effect of doing so is cancelled. There was an incident in Lord Krishna's life that happened after the Mahabharata War, when millions of people were killed. There was nobody left except seven people on the Pandava side and three people on the Kaurava side. The Kauravas were the bad guys; the Pandavas were the good guys.

At the end of the war, the Pandava king Yudhisthira, was very sad. He was a wise person, but he was still very sad. After all, if we were responsible for killing three million people, we would be a little sad also. He went and asked Sri Bhagavan, "Lord, I'm feeling miserable. Everybody—all my relatives, all my friends, all the kings—everybody has died except for a few people. How can I get rid of this feeling?"

Bhagavan said, "There is a way. Do the *Ashwamedha Yagna*, the horse sacrifice."

So he and his four brothers did the sacrifice, and it was very grand. They got together all the wealth they could and gave it away at the end. Bhagavan said, "Listen, this sacrifice will be completed only when you hear a divine bell ringing in the sky. You won't see it; you'll only hear it. That will mean it is complete, finished, perfect."

After they gave away all their wealth, invited sadhus and holy men from all over and fed them. Still no bell. They didn't know what was the matter. They thought, 'Maybe because we didn't feed Sri Bhagavan Himself it is not ringing,' so they asked Him, "Please Lord, come and have lunch." But even after He had His lunch, no bell. They didn't know what was the matter. "Bhagavan, what is the matter? There is no bell. Are we doing something wrong?"

Krishna said, "Yes, there is one sadhu in the forest. He eats only dried leaves. You should go invite him for lunch, and when he eats, the bell will ring."

They sent a messenger to call the sadhu. They are royalty, after all. They are proud. They are not going to go themselves to a sadhu. However, that is the problem. Forget about the bell. It is not going to ring.

The messenger went to the sadhu "Swamiji, the king wants you to eat lunch. Please come."

"Sorry, I'm otherwise engaged. I'm having a feast today of dried leaves, the ones that fell off the tree."

They went back. They told the king and his brothers. They thought, 'Because we are proud he didn't come,' so they went running to see him.

They said, "Swami, please come for food in the palace today."

The sadhu said, "I'll come under one condition. You must give me the merit of a hundred and one yagnas (sacrifices).

They exclaimed, "How can we do that? We don't even have one to our credit! How are we going to give a hundred and one to you?"

He said, "Okay. Bye-bye."

So they left. They told their wife Draupadi, "What a calamity! We did this sacrifice and we can't even get the bell to ring."

Draupadi said, "Don't worry. I'll cook food with my own hands and take it."

So she cooked a beautiful meal and went barefoot all the way to the ashram and put the food before the swami and said,

"Swami, please eat this food."

He said, "Only if you give me the merit from a hundred and one yagnas."

She replied, "Swami, the scriptures say that if a person comes to a mahatma with love and devotion, they have performed one yagna every step of the way. So, you can take a hundred and one out of all that I just earned, because I must have taken many more than a hundred and one steps to get here."

What to do? He had to agree. He went to the palace and sat down. There were about twenty-seven food items. He put everything on the leaf and mixed it all into one big lump and ate it. Draupadi was thinking, 'Wow, this poor fellow has never eaten decent food in his life.'

After he finished his food, the bell didn't ring. They all looked at Bhagavan. "Bhagavan, what is this? You said that if he ate the food the bell would ring. What is the matter?"

Bhagavan said, "I'll tell you what is the matter. Draupadi's mind is the matter, because she thinks this sadhu has never had good food and that is why he is acting like this. However, a sadhu is a person who lives in God. He doesn't live in the food. His mind is tasting the inner presence of God. He doesn't want to be distracted from that, so he just eats the food as a medicine. That is why he is not interested in the taste. It is just a medicine to feed the disease of hunger. It is to give him strength to continue his sadhana."

Then Draupadi realized her mistake and prayed, "Bhagavan, O Bhagavan, please forgive me for my pride and ignorance."

Then the bell rang, 'ding, ding, a-ling.' So give, but don't have any pride when giving.

We still have three more questions to be answered, three small ones, and one very big one.

Question: Many people tell me that Amma is their Guru. Does Amma have to tell them that such is the case, or could one just choose her to be their Guru? Does Amma have to say she is our Guru, or is it enough if we say Amma is our Guru?

Answer: The sun shines on everything and everybody equally. It doesn't belong to anybody. It doesn't have to say, "I'm shining on you, I'm not shining on you." If it is not shining on something, it means that thing isn't standing in the sunlight. It is in the shade.

In the same way, a Realized person like Amma is a Universal Presence. It is there for everybody. Amma does not have any particularity or specialty towards anybody or anything. Yet, if we want to get the warmth of the sun, we have to stand in the sunlight. In the same way, if we want the benefit of Amma's presence, we've got to get as close as possible to her. Not just physically. Physically to be close to Amma is also very helpful, but mentally we have got to become close to her. It is not that Amma makes herself our Guru; we desire and accept her as our Guru. That must come from our side, not from Amma's side. She cannot teach us anything, she cannot show us the way, she can't guide us, unless we want to be guided by her. We have to make the connection. She is always waiting for us, but she is not a dictator. She is not going to force anything on anybody.

Destiny plays a role in who is to be our Guru. We may come to Amma, but we may not feel that she is our Guru. She may not be our guide or refuge. If it is already decided who is one's Guru even at the time of birth, perhaps that is the reason; nobody is to blame for that. Even then, anybody can get the benefit of Amma's presence.

Even if we accept Amma as our Guru, if we want to get the maximum benefit from being her disciple, we should get initiated by her. At that time, Amma transfers some of her spiritual power into us like lighting a small fire from a big fire. Unless that happens, we stay like an unlit fire for a very long time. Initiation is a means to lighting our spiritual fire.

It is not enough to just say, "Amma is my Guru." If we have a guru, then we must live as a disciple. There are many devotees of Amma. Anybody who is got a little faith in Amma, who loves Amma, is a devotee of Amma. But a disciple is something else. A disciple is someone who reflects the Guru, whose life is moulded by the Guru's example, who follows the teachings of the Guru. We must study Amma's teachings, associate with her, and mould our life to Amma's ideals and words. Then only can we be a disciple and say that Amma is our Guru. Otherwise, it is just words and that is not enough. Anyone can say "I am a king" or "I am a queen" without being one. If we really mould ourself to Amma's teachings, then we've got to become an instrument of Amma's grace. It has to happen.

Story of Saint Eknath's Disciple, Puranpoli

Puranpoli was a child living in the same village in Maharasthra as the great saint Eknath. It is interesting how Puranpoli got his name. There is a kind of sweet called *puranpoli*, and this boy used to love these sweets. He would always nag his mother, "Mommy, make some puranpoli, I want some more." That is all he thought of. Of course, little kids always want something like that, but he was obsessed with this; it was the only thing he could think of. He didn't want to go to school; he only wanted to eat this sweet. The child was also very dull. He couldn't learn anything. But he was very sharp when it came to eating puranpoli. Finally, his mother got fed up with him and exclaimed, "I'm not going to give him anything. He is useless. He is good for nothing but eating puranpoli." She went to Eknath's house, as he was also a householder, and said, "Mahatmaji, please take this dullard from my hands. All he wants to do is eat puranpoli."

Eknath said, "We also make it here in our house. We feed it to God as the food offering during the puja, so he will be happy here."

Eknath tried to teach the boy the alphabet, but nothing would go into his head, not even 'a', 'aa', 'e', 'ee'. So Eknath kept quiet and fed the boy as much puranpoli as he wanted.

This went on for some months, and then gradually, Puranpoli got a taste for Eknath's company. He used to sit and watch the puja and attend the bhajans and listen to Eknath give satsang. Slowly, Puranpoli got very attached to Eknath and took refuge in him, following him around, and serving him. Soon, Eknath became everything to him.

Eknath was getting old. At that time, he was writing a commentary on the *Ramayana*. Since Eknath was a true mahatma, his commentary was superb, but he realized that it was the time for him to leave his body. He couldn't find anybody to finish the commentary, so he called Puranpoli and said, "You finish the commentary." Puranpoli agreed. He was very happy. But what did he know? All he knew was eating and being with Eknath. After Eknath passed away, Puranpoli wrote the rest of the commentary, and to this day, people who read it say that it is indistinguishable from the first part which Eknath wrote. He received the grace of Eknath just by his association, love and guidance.

Through their constant association with her, Amma's disciples become totally different people than who they were when they came to her. So if you want to be a disciple of Amma, it means not just being attached to her, but following her teachings and trying to mould your life to them. You can't say, "I'm a disciple of Amma's and she is my Guru," and live in such a way that doesn't reflect that fact. But to answer the question, Amma won't make you a disciple. You have to do the work. Amma will show the way if you take refuge in her.

Spiritual Actions are an Investment

Question: It would be very interesting to hear about the different spiritual qualities and how one could cultivate them.

Answer: In the *Bhagavad Gita*, Sri Bhagavan tells what the spiritual qualities are. It is a big list.

> "Fearlessness, purity of heart, steadfastness in knowledge and in yoga, charity, self-restraint, worship, study of the scriptures, austerity, uprightness, harmlessness, truth, absence of anger, renunciation, serenity, absence of calumny, compassion to creatures, uncovetousness, gentleness, modesty, absence of fickleness, energy, forgiveness, fortitude, absence of hatred, absence of pride, these belong to one born for a divine lot, oh Arjuna."
>
> —Ch.16, v.1

If we have all these qualities, then we have the good fortune to have been born with a spiritual nature, and that will lead us to God-realization. Having the opposite, or demonic qualities will take us away from God-realization.

All living beings have one thing in common: everybody wants to be happy. This is one of a few basic truths that we need to hear again and again. Spiritual teachers put it in different packages, that is all.

Everybody wants to be happy. The only difference between spiritual people and others in this regard is that spiritual people investigate all the means of happiness that the world presents and come to the conclusion that such means and ends are not good enough. They don't last, and they cause us to get immersed in complicated and frequently painful situations. Spiritually-minded people want something more lasting, more stable, more intense and thrilling. Worldly happiness is not enough for them.

Somehow they come across the teachings of mahatmas like Amma who say, "You don't have to be satisfied with worldly pleasure. In fact, if you're unsatisfied with that, it is a good sign. Don't stop there. When you've reached the stage where you're not getting the happiness that you want from things, seek what is beyond even that."

What is beyond worldly happiness? *Atmananda*, the bliss of our own Self, the bliss that is within us, but which is completely hidden now. The only time we experience it is when we go to sleep, in deep, dreamless sleep. It is hidden by our thoughts. We've got to try to reduce our thoughts so our inner bliss can shine forth.

Most people are not willing to invest their time in that. They want something now. Suppose we give a chocolate candy and a gold coin to a little child. What is going to happen? The child is going to take the chocolate. He is not going to care about the gold coin. He doesn't even know that he could buy many pieces of chocolate for the gold coin. He just wants the immediate thing right in front of him.

Most of us are like that; we're not really willing to invest our time and energy to get that bliss. We may hear about it, we may believe in it, but we don't really want to do what is needed to uncover the treasure that is within us. However, ultimately, that is what has to be done. We come into this world again and again to learn certain lessons through pleasure and pain, and finally turn towards the ultimate thing, our inner bliss.

Amma says if we want to attain lasting bliss, we've got to do sadhana. Amma's words ultimately point to this: we must do sadhana to evolve spiritually and become fit for God's grace. She doesn't talk much philosophy; she is very practical. We must purify our thoughts. Our mind has to be thoroughly cleansed. We have to cultivate good thoughts and resist and destroy negative ones. This is possible through meditation, bhajan, etc.

A spiritual person has to be like a business person—always profit-oriented. Every minute, we've got to be thinking, 'Am I gaining or am I losing?' Always think like that every moment, every word we speak, every movement of our eyes, every thought in our mind, every action of our body. 'Am I gaining spiritually or am I losing? Am I going forward towards the goal of atmananda, or am I going away from it?' Remember that everything we do, good or bad, is going to be deposited in our unseen spiritual bank account.

All of us have a spiritual bank account. Wise people encourage us to fill that account with good thoughts, words and deeds, which are called *punyam* in Sanskrit. Every time that we repeat a mantra or say a kind word, some punyam or credit goes into our subtle piggy bank. Every time that we say something nasty, we get debited. Our punyam and *papam* (debit) are the only things we take with us when we leave our body behind in death and proceed to a subtler existence. However much we accumulate in this world, we have to leave every single thing behind. However, what we do take is this: the good and the bad actions, the results of which will become the pleasures and pains in our next birth.

In any plane of existence in the entire creation, our good and bad actions are valid currency.

Punyam can be material or spiritual. Material comforts, wealth, power, beauty, health and power are the result of past material punyam. Charitable acts bring these results about. Spiritual punyam results in spiritual opportunities and conducive mental tendencies. It is the cause for our being interested in spirituality and of obtaining satsang. How did we come to Amma? How did we get the chance to read spiritual books? All of that is because of our past spiritual punyam. It is very important to do punyam. We want to have the company of devotees or mahatmas. We don't want bad company. The worst suffering for a devotee or a spiritual-minded person is to have no spiritual company, having to live in the midst of completely worldly people.

We should try to get out of the mess that we're in, being born into this world and having to die. Nobody wants to die, but still, whether we want to or not, we're going to. So we have to take steps so at least it doesn't happen again, even though it is going to happen at the end of this life. We've got to make spiritual progress as fast as we can. You've got to do punyam, you've got to get more and more punyam through mantra japa, bhajan, satsang, meditation, and so on. But even then, that won't take us all the way to the goal. We need to attain Self-realization. We should experience the direct knowledge of Brahman, our True Nature. Spiritual punyam will lead us to that place, so that our mind becomes pure and circumstances become conducive for that. Many of us have read the *Vivekachudamani* by Sri Sankaracharya. In that, he says,

> "Liberation is not to be attained except through the well earned merits of millions of births."

Sri Vidyaranya, another Vedantic sage, says,

> "The mind continues to be fixed in the Paramatman in the state of samadhi as a result of the effort of will made prior to its achievement and helped by the merits of previous births and the strong impression created through constant efforts (at getting into samadhi)."
>
> —*Panchadasi, Ch.1, v.57*

This is very important. Constant effort and meritorious deeds are needed to attain the Supreme State.

Wake up From the Sleep of Maya

All the Indian scriptures, and mahatmas like Amma, say that we are not what we imagine. Though we seem to be awake, we are actually sleeping—the long sleep of Maya. We are dreaming that our body and mind are our self, and the world that we live in is real. In fact, our life is a long dream in a long dream world. When we go into deep, dreamless sleep, we contact our real Self. We love that state so much that we long to experience it every night. At that time, there is not the stress of body-and world-consciousness; there is only peace. Even though awareness of that is only dim, we do recall it as blissful and restful. Then our desires and fears give rise to our dreaming state and ultimately wake us up. Mahatmas say that it is possible to enjoy the blissfulness of deep sleep even while awake. With the dawning of the experience of our True Nature, we will begin to feel that peace. For that to happen, we must purify our mind through the cultivation of 'divine' qualities as told to Arjuna by Lord Krishna in the *Bhagavad Gita*.

The first quality is fearlessness. The root cause of fear is our identification with the body and the resulting experience that 'I' and not-'I' are different. We feel threatened by an unfriendly world. When we are identified with a body, then we feel that there are things that aren't ourself. Due to that feeling, desire and fear arise.

We become afraid of physical pain, mental suffering, anything that is painful, anything that is not pleasant; even boredom is painful. We want positive pleasure, positive happiness. When we go to sleep, in deep sleep, is there any pain? Is there any fear? No. Why not? Because there is no body-consciousness. That is the only time that there is absolutely no fear. Someone could be standing by our body with a knife and we wouldn't feel the slightest bit of fear because we have no body-consciousness.

How to get rid of fear? Somebody may be afraid of failing in school, somebody may be afraid of their father or their mother; everybody has some fear or other. We can get rid of it. Take refuge in God or in your Guru.

Amma says,

> "Surrender removes all fear and tension. Surrender leads one to peace and bliss. Where there is surrender, there is no fear, and vice versa. Where there is surrender, there is love and compassion, whereas fear results in hatred and enmity. But to surrender, one needs a lot of courage, the courage to give up oneself. It demands a daring attitude to sacrifice one's ego. Surrender means welcoming and accepting everything without the least feeling of sorrow or disappointment."

Many people pray only when they feel helpless. Maybe that is why some difficult situations come up for them that cause them to be afraid—so that they will pray, so that they will look within a bit. A grandmother asked her grandchild, "Did you say your prayers last night?"

"Yes, grandma, every night I say my prayers."

"And do you say them every morning?"

"No, grandma, I'm not afraid in the morning."

Some people become terminally ill and go through different stages. The first stage is fear, and then there is the denial stage, "No, it is not going to happen to me." Then anger, "Why should this happen to me?" Finally, they reach the stage of acceptance and surrender, and then the mind becomes peaceful. Many people in that condition have a very peaceful death. That acceptance, that surrender, is one way to get rid of fear.

We should try to feel that, 'Whatever is happening to me is all God's will. I seek refugee in God or Guru. Nothing will happen to me except what is for my good.' Try to not combat it; try to accept it. Don't fight it; just try to accept the situation and offer your fear to God or Guru.

Once there were two men who were going through a field when a bull started chasing them. Wild bulls don't like people very much. So, this bull started chasing them and they were running and running. The bull was catching up to them, and they couldn't reach the fence. So one of them turned to the other and said, "We've had it. Nothing can save us. The bull is about to catch us. Say a prayer. At least now, say a prayer."

The other man said, "What prayer? I have never prayed in my life. What am I supposed to say, especially for this occasion? I don't have any prayers for this occasion."

The first man said, "Never mind, the bull is about to catch up with us. Any prayer will do, any prayer is fine."

"Well, there was a prayer that my father used to say before meals. I'll say that one."

"What was it?"

"For what we are about to receive, O Lord, may we be grateful!"

That is one way to get rid of fear—praying like that. Be grateful for whatever happens. Give up fear and accept everything as it is. Be even-minded.

One disciple of a Guru was huddling around a fire with the other disciples and said, "I know what to do. Our Guru taught me what to do if it is very cold."

"Really? What?"

"Keep warm!"

"That is brilliant! And what if you can't keep warm?"

"Oh, then he also told me what to do."

"Really? What is that?"

"Freeze!"

So that is what the Guru teaches, not just common sense, but accepting the situation, and then fear will go.

When I was thinking about this subject of fear, I was reminded of my own experiences with fear. I think the time I felt the most fear was before I came to Amma. I used to walk around the Arunachala hill. I used to like to walk around it at night. People do it as a worship or meditation. I used to do it as a combination of both, imagining that the mountain was Lord Shiva, and I was keeping Him on my right side while walking. This can be very distracting during the daytime because of the traffic. At night there is nobody around, but there are also no lights. It was a country road and that area is full of scorpions and cobras.

Yet at the same time, I wanted to get the benefit of walking at night. I wouldn't take a flashlight because I thought, 'Why take a flashlight? God will protect me.' I would sometimes hear the jackals howling in the distance, near the hill. First I would think, 'Are they hungry? Why are they making that noise? There are so many of them! I wonder if they eat people?' I'd feel a little afraid then. I'd think, 'When am I going to step on a cobra? When is a scorpion going to sting me?' I would walk barefoot; when one is doing an act of worship, one should remove one's shoes.

Soon I noticed I was getting very distracted with these thoughts. I scolded myself, 'What is this? I surrendered myself to God a long time ago and came to India. Why am I worrying? What is my faith? What is my level of surrender? Forget it! What is the use of being afraid? Whatever is my fate, my *prarabdha*, whatever is my Guru's or God's will is going to happen to me, whether or not I worry about it. I'm just wasting energy, spoiling my mind, defeating the purpose of my life by being worried. Being afraid is useless, because there is nothing that I can do about it.'

Then my mind would become peaceful and everything would be all right. It was very strange because, many times, I almost stepped on snakes. They used to jump away just before I was about to step on them, but I never got bit by one. And many times, after resting by the roadside and getting up, I'd find a scorpion right next to my leg. If I had just rolled over, I would have been stung. Those were big black scorpions that reminded one of lobsters. They are called hill scorpions because they live up there and come down to the plains when it rains. But nothing ever happened to me other than a mosquito bite or a bee sting.

One day, I was sitting on the edge of some steps while talking to somebody who was behind me. I felt something slide across the back of my feet. I looked down, but there was nothing there. I looked on one side, and there was nothing there either. Until then, I wasn't afraid. Then I looked on the other side, and there was a seven-foot long cobra going into the bushes. I jumped up, shouting, "Snake! Snake!" What is the use of getting afraid when the cause is gone? So, if it was my fate to have been bitten, it would have happened at that moment for sure! Our prarabdha or fate, or God's will, is already decided at the time of birth. Whatever is going to happen is going to happen; we can't do anything about that. We've got to do what we have to do in life. Take refuge in God or Guru and then, lead a life without worry. Our mind will gradually become peaceful, and slowly, we'll go towards the spiritual goal.

The Greatness of Sages

"In the depths of the sea, there are no waves. They are only in shallow areas near the shoreline. Those who have attained Perfection will be calm. People with little knowledge, after reading two or three books, will create problems."

—*Amma*

Some of us have seen how people who have read a few books come to Amma to display their knowledge. Either they try to show how knowledgeable they are or even worse, try to teach Amma something. It is a very sad thing to see. They seem to think that book knowledge is a great thing.

Getting Tuned Through Guruseva

Many years ago, before Amma was well-known, a swami from another ashram came to see her. He gave a lecture to Amma about the intricacies of Vedanta philosophy. After patiently listening to him, she said,

"Well, more important than Vedanta is *seva*."

The swami said, "No, that is not correct. Study of Vedanta is most important."

Amma said, "No, if a person sincerely does Guruseva, they will become tuned to God. However much Vedanta one practices, one may not get that tuning." Saying so, she sat for a moment with her eyes closed. A minute later, a brahmacharini who was serving Amma came running up with a glass of tea. Amma asked her,

"Why did you bring this tea now? I don't want tea."

"Amma, I thought that you said that you wanted tea; I heard in my mind as if you said you wanted tea."

"In fact, I did want the tea, but not for me; it was for the swami."

The swami was amazed that there was a person so tuned to Amma's thoughts who could respond like this. This is one of the values of Guruseva and the devotional path; we get mentally tuned to the Guru's mind that is tuned to God.

The Self or Atma is not somewhere that we have to reach. It is not up in Heaven. Nor do we have to go around the world to find it. However, we may have to serve a true Guru. We may have to learn so many things. But we should always remember that what we're trying to reach is our own Self, our own real nature. It is something that is hidden now by our thoughts, by our feelings. To realize that, we have to go through the process. Don't think it's going to be something we are going to find somewhere else.

The Truth is Already Within Us

There was a man who kept having the same dream. What was it? That he should go to Washington D.C. He lived in Los Angeles. His name was John Doe. Every night in the dream, a voice would tell him, "Go to Washington D.C. Go to the Pentagon. Just in front of the Pentagon, there is a big bridge, and under that bridge there is a treasure. If you dig up that treasure, you'll never have to work again for the rest of your life." He was a very poor man; he was struggling for his existence. So he kept ignoring this dream, thinking that, after all, it is just a dream. Nevertheless, the same dream kept coming again and again.

Finally he decided, 'All right, I'll somehow go.' He saved up his money and went all the way to Washington D.C. Sure enough, right in front of the Pentagon was a bridge. Unfortunately, many soldiers guarded the bridge, since they didn't want any one to sneak into the Pentagon.

He was very discouraged. He would look at the bridge and then go away. The next day, he would look at the bridge, then look around, and go away. Some of the soldiers were feeling suspicious about him. "What is this man doing here?" Finally they called him one day. They said, "Sir, why are you coming here every day and looking at the bridge like that?"

The man replied, "I feel kind of embarrassed to tell you this, but I had a dream. It kept coming again and again, and I was told that if I dig under this bridge, I would find a treasure."

"You must be joking! An intelligent man like you cares about such dreams? You came all the way here for that? You could have stayed comfortably in Los Angeles. You know, I have also been having a dream, now that you mention it. It is very similar, and if I listened to that dream, I would have to go to Los Angeles," said a guard.

"Really, what is the dream?"

The soldier said, "I'm having this dream every night since about a week. It tells me that there is this man in Los Angeles; his name is John Doe, and in his backyard under the tree in the northeast corner, there is a treasure. And if I would dig there, I would never have to work for the rest of my life; I'd find this treasure."

The man was stunned. He said, "Thank you very much. It is a good thing that you didn't go to Los Angeles. After all, how are you going to find John Doe there? There must be tens of thousands of John Does." He went back to his house, and in the backyard, in the corner, under the tree, he dug there and found the treasure. But he couldn't have found the treasure unless he went all the way to Washington D.C., even though it was in his own backyard! He had to be told where to find it.

We are trying to experience God-realization. It is within us, but unless there is a great deal of hard work invested, we can't experience it. It is not so easy. Somebody asked Amma, "Why can't I experience samadhi? Why is it so difficult?"

Amma replied, "You've got a lot of images in your mind. You've read a lot of books. You have many ideas, so your mind is filled with images and thoughts. If you want to attain samadhi, your mind has to become emptied of all those things, and then what is left is the samadhi state. Your attention has to be shifted from your thoughts to the awareness that reveals the thoughts. If you can't do that, you need to do a lot of mantra japa."

We need to understand this principle. All spiritual practice is to reduce thoughts to one thought, the thought of God. Then the experience of awareness will begin to emerge. For highly intellectual people, this task is very difficult. They are always trying to understand everything.

The Simplest May Be the Smartest

Sometimes simple-hearted people who don't seem to be very intelligent, are the ones that progress spiritually without much difficulty.

One day, a truck was driving along; it was one of those big trucks, an 18 wheeler, that one frequently sees on the highway. When it was going under an underpass, it got stuck. It was just a few inches taller than the overpass and got wedged in there. Everybody was trying to get the truck out. They pushed and pulled, but it was no use. They even called the police and the road maintenance crews. Nobody could figure it out. They thought that they might have to destroy part of the overbridge to get the truck out of there. All the experts were consulted, but nobody could come up with a solution. It was really jammed in there.

There was a little kid who was standing by the road watching the whole scene. He went over to the crowd and started pulling on the jacket of one of the experts. Irritated by the boy, the man said, "Just leave me alone. I'm very busy. Can't you see it is an important thing that is going on here?"

The kid said, "I want to tell you something." He just kept pulling, and finally, the man got fed up.

"All right, tell me what you want to tell me. What is it?"

"I have a suggestion."

"You have a suggestion? What do you know? You are only six years old."

"I know that, but anyhow, I've got a suggestion; will you just listen to me?"

"Alright."

The boy said, "I suggest you let some of the air out of the tires." None of the experts had even thought of that. Sometimes the simple people are the ones that are the real winners, not the smart or clever ones.

> "The waves of the sea cannot be destroyed. Likewise, the thoughts of the mind cannot be completely eliminated. Once the mind gains depth and breadth, thought waves will subside naturally."

Detachment Stills the Mind

We may not be able to make the mind completely calm. We may not be able to stop all the thoughts. What we can do is distance ourself from them; try to be more of a witness to the mind instead of taking part in its endless monkey business. It will gradually slow down, and we will feel an expansive awareness quite separate from it.

For example, suppose an argument is going on. We also get involved and are not aware of anything that is going on except that argument. We're completely absorbed into the heat of the argument. On the other hand, if we are a disinterested observer, we can see the argument and also the world. We are not involved. Similarly, through meditation, japa and Vedantic practice, we can emotionally detach ourselves to some extent from the restless mind. That detachment brings about a kind of calmness. The fuel for the heated mind gets taken away. Emotional attachment makes the mind restless. When it is not attached, then it starts to calm down.

Purification of the Ego

"Children, both the real and the unreal are contained in a seed. So what is real? The real thing is the seed. The unreal thing is the husk around the seed. When a seed is sown, the husk will crack and become one with the soil. The essence of the seed will sprout and grow. Similarly, both real and unreal are within us. If we live while paying attention to the real, nothing will bother us. We'll become expansive. If we resort to the unreal, we cannot grow."

Amma is talking about expansiveness, how being immersed in what is unreal contracts us. It takes away our peace and our happiness. Everybody is a mixture of real and unreal. What is real and what unreal? The real us, the Atma, the 'I', the awareness in us, is real. But the body is not real because it is not permanent; it changes all the time and finally perishes. Our constantly changing mind is also part of the unreal. But in the case of the mind, it is a mixture of qualities, some of which will lead us to the real, and some of which will take us away from the real. Some of them reflect the light, just like a mirror, and some of them cloud the light, like mud or dirty water.

As mentioned earlier, in the *Bhagavad Gita*, Sri Bhagavan says that these different qualities are called the divine qualities and the demonic qualities; we should study this very closely. We should read it every day, and try to cultivate the divine ones, and reduce or get rid of the demonic ones so that our real nature can shine.

The Demonic Qualities

So what are the demonic qualities? Ostentation, arrogance, self-conceit, anger, insolence and ignorance. Bhagavan says the divine nature leads to Self-realization or liberation from the cycle of birth and death, and the demonic nature leads to rebirth and suffering. It is not so easy to cultivate the divine qualities. We would like to grow spiritually, but we may not be aware of the fact that for spiritual growth, our ego must be purified. The pure ego can reflect the Atmic consciousness. Hearing and understanding this is one thing, but putting it into practice is quite another. Even a little bit of practice is difficult.

Once there was a mahatma who used to give beautiful talks. Many people would hang onto his words of inspiration. But there was one man in the audience who would always make fun of the mahatma and pick on him. He'd try to find some fault in his personality or in his way of talking. He'd insult him and abuse him in front of everybody. The disciples of the mahatma used to be very irritated with him. They wished that this man would not come around, but he continued to come every day. The mahatma was very friendly and loving to this man.

The disciples started calling this man 'the devil.' One day 'the devil' died. The disciples were very happy. Of course, they didn't act as if they were very happy, but in their minds, they were. Everybody went to the funeral, but only the mahatma was weeping. He was genuinely sorrowful. The disciples asked him, "Swami, why are you crying? You must be feeling so bad about what the fate of this man will be. He must be in some terrible place now for acting the way he did."

The mahatma replied, "Not at all! Why should I cry about that? This man has gone to Heaven. I am crying for myself, because all of you praise me day and night and thereby increase my ego. He was the only one that used to cut me down; he was the only one that would keep my ego under control. Now that he is gone, who is going to do that for me?"

Most of us want praise. We want appreciation. We want others to feed our ego. But a mahatma doesn't want that. He is very happy with that which gives him a chance to keep his ego small and allows God-consciousness to blossom in him. This is what Amma is saying—turn away from the unreal, the ego, so that the Atma can shine. A real Guru like Amma knows what to do and when to make us grow.

Story of the King who Served Kabir

There once was a Persian king who had developed real detachment and truly wanted to experience God, so he went to Kasi (Benares), where the famous saint Kabir was living. On finding Kabir, the saint said, "After all, what do I have in common with you? You are a king. I'm just a poor weaver. I think you have come to the wrong place."

The king said, "No. I know you are a Realized person, a mahatma. I want your grace. I want initiation."

Kabir replied, "I'll think about it."

The king started serving Kabir's family. He used to bring water and wash the clothes, cut the vegetables and do all the heavy work. In those days, there was no water tap that one could just open. One would have to walk a long distance to a well and draw the water. For all their bathing, cooking and washing needs, he'd spend most of his day carrying water. Six years went by like this; he was living in a back room of the house, in just one small cell. Six years!

Finally, Kabir's wife said to her husband, "Why don't you give him initiation? He's been living here like a servant for six years now. All the other people who came here were given initiation so quickly. You're not giving him anything. You're treating him so badly."

Sometimes people say, "My son or daughter's been living in Amritapuri for five years cutting vegetables. What is the use of such a life?" Well, spiritual life is not like worldly life. Sometimes by cutting vegetables for five years, one can progress a lot spiritually.

A man went to a Guru desiring instruction. The Guru said, "Thou art That."

"Is that all?" asked the man. He was not satisfied and went to another Guru who understood his condition.

"Well, you will have to work very hard before I will instruct you," said this Guru. The disciple was ready to do anything. "All right, the only thing that you have to do is shovel cow dung for twelve years," said the Guru and gave the man a shovel. After twelve years, the Guru called the man and told him, "Thou art That." The disciple immediately realized Brahman as his own Self.

The disciple was always shovelling cow dung ten hours a day and started seeing everything as God, just from shovelling the cow dung. It wasn't in the cow dung. It wasn't in the shovel. It was in the faith and attitude that he was doing guruseva; he was always thinking of his Guru. So, he started seeing everything as filled with his Guru's presence.

Kabir said to his wife, "You don't understand."

His wife said, "No. I can see that this man is humble; he is so meek. He does whatever we say. He doesn't want anything. He is eating the poor food that we are eating. He is living on the cement floor in a cell. I know he is ready for initiation."

Kabir replied, "All right, call him here, but before he gets here, call the servant lady and tell her that when he comes in the door, she should be sweeping there, and as soon as he walks in, she should whack him with the broom and shout abuse at him."

So, she called the servant lady who started sweeping the floor. When the king walked in, the lady whacked him with the broom. "You rascal, why did you come in here? I'm trying to sweep the floor. Get out of here!" she shouted.

The king looked at her and said, "If I were still the king, you know what I would do to you? I'd teach you a good lesson." He didn't say anything after that. He came and sat in front of Kabir. Kabir said, "You can go." He went away. Kabir smiled at his wife. The wife couldn't say anything.

Six more years passed. Now twelve years were over. Traditionally, it is told that for twelve years, one must serve a Guru. Only then will one be ready for real spirituality, for the real thing. Before that, it is all preparation. So, twelve years passed and then Kabir called his wife. "Call the king. I want to initiate him today."

"What do you mean? He is exactly the same person as he was six years ago. He is still so humble and meek, and does whatever we say," said the wife.

Kabir said, "You can't see the man's mind. You don't see anything beyond the body. You can't see what's inside. I can see. Call him. He is ready now."

"I don't believe it."

"Okay, call the servant again. Tell her to beat him up with the broom this time when he comes in."

So, when the king came in, the servant lady started beating him up with the broom and shouted at him. She was screaming and pushed him out of the door. Then he came back in and bowed down. He touched her feet. He said, "Thank you, Mother, I really needed that."

Kabir called him over. He just gazed at him with a kind look of compassion and the king went into samadhi. He didn't receive any mantra into his ear. Just a look, because when we're ripe, nothing else is necessary. Even the Guru's mere presence will be enough to make us go into samadhi. This is what happens if we always embrace the real.

Amma's Song Ananda Veedhi

> "For one who has known Reality, the whole world is his wealth. He cannot see anything as different from his own Self."

This is from a song Amma wrote called *'Ananda Veedhi'*. It is about her experience of Self-realization. In the song, she says that the Divine Mother appeared before her and...

> "Smiling, the Divine Mother became an Effulgence and merged in me. My mind blossomed, bathed in the many-hued light of Divinity. And the events of millions of years gone by rose up within me."

A vision of the Divine Mother appeared to Amma. It then became an effulgence and merged into her. Then what happened? Her mind became illumined and the knowledge of all of her past millions of births' experiences dawned on her.

Perhaps for some souls, at that time, one realizes how futile it was that one was repeatedly born and died and did the same things again and again. Tremendous detachment from the cycle of living and dying may arise resulting in the withdrawal of the mind completely into the Self and one finally wakes up from this long dream of birth, death and rebirth.

> "All these events of millions of years rose up within. Then seeing nothing as apart from my own Self, a Unity, and merging in Her, the Divine Mother, I renounced all sense of enjoyment."

Normally, we see everything as separate from ourself or "I." We endlessly seek happiness in the objective world. Unfortunately, our happiness does not last long and this process of seeking happiness starts all over again. We die and eventually come back here to do the same things again. Such is life.

Amma is saying that when she woke up from the dream of duality, she saw that what seemed to be "I" and "not-I" was one Unity. When we dream, we are the seer experiencing a world which seems objective and real. But when we wake up, what happens? That world and all the beings in it cease to exist. The fact is, that everything in that world including ourself was a projection of our mind. It was made of our thoughts. Even the God in that world was our own mental image. Of course, at that time, we were totally unaware of that. We felt that we and the world were real. Similarly, Amma realized that everything was her Self. Then there was no question of enjoying anymore, because, what was there to enjoy and why? She experienced or realized that she is the Self, and that Self is Supreme Bliss.

This is what Amma means when she says, "For one who has known Reality, the whole world is his wealth. He can't see anything as different from his own Self." He doesn't want anything.

He doesn't need anything, because everything is himself. He has woken up from the dream. Such people may appear to be beggars, as if they have nothing, but really, they are the rich ones, because they don't need anything. They are truly independent.

Alexander Meets a Really Great Man

Alexander the Great (336-323 B.C.) was considered great in the eyes of himself and his followers. He conquered many lands and killed or enslaved countless people in his ambition to conquer the entire known world. I guess that was felt to be great at that time.

After conquering all the lands to the east of Greece, Alexander reached India, the land of the truly great sages who had conquered their egos and experienced the Reality, the source of the mind.

Dandi Swami was a sage whom Alexander heard about when he was near Taxila. He then sent his friend Onescratus to bring the swami to him. When Onescratus encountered Dandi Swami in the forest, he gave him the message that Alexander the Great, Son of Zeus, had ordered him to come to him. "He will give you gold and other rewards, but if you refuse, he may behead you."

When Dandi Swami heard that, he did not even raise his head and replied, lying in his bed of leaves, "God, the Great King is not a source of violence but provider of water, food, light and life. Your king, who loves violence and who is mortal, cannot be God. Even if you take away my head, you cannot take away my soul which will depart to my God and leave this body like one throws away old garments. We do not love gold nor fear death. So your king has nothing to offer that I may need. Go and tell your king: Dandi will not come to you. If he needs Dandi, let him come here."

Alexander went to the forest to meet the swami and sat before him for more than an hour. The *avadhuta* was stark naked. He was lying under a tree sunbathing. As soon as Alexander saw his glowing face, he fell in love with him. His divine effulgence was overpowering. Even the most beautiful or handsome person was dull compared to that sadhu.

Then Dandi Swami asked him, "Why have you come to me? I have nothing to offer you. I have no thought of pleasure or gold, I love God and despise death. Whereas you love pleasure, gold and kill people, fear death and despise God."

Alexander replied, "I have come to learn wisdom from you. Please come with me back to Greece."

The mahatma looked up at him and said, "This world is in me. It can't hold me. It is in me. The universe, Greece, and everything is in me. The stars are in me, the sun is in me, the moon is in me. Where can I go?"

Alexander said, "I'll give you anything you want. I'll have many people serve you. You can have delicious food and anything else you may desire."

The mahatma laughed and said, "The brilliance in the diamonds that you are wearing and the brilliance in the sun, the lustre in the moon and the twinkling stars—all these things, all the charm in the world—do you know where it comes from? It comes from me. It would be beneath my dignity if, after lending my brilliance to all these things, I went running after them. I would be like a beggar. I am not going to become a beggar. I'm a king. I'm the King of the Universe. Goodbye."

Alexander was impressed. He didn't understand what he heard, but he was impressed by the holy presence of the mahatma. Such is a person who has realized the Self, who sees everything as himself. All the wealth of the world is just his Self.

Story of a Black Boy and a Black Balloon

There was a little black boy from a very poor family. One day, he went to the circus fairgrounds and saw a balloon seller there. This balloon seller really knew how to sell balloons. He'd cut the string of one balloon and let it fly up in the air. Everybody would see this balloon flying up into the air and then want to get a balloon. So, while the little boy was looking, the man cut one red one, and it went flying up. He cut a yellow balloon, and it went flying up. He cut one of the white balloons, and it went flying up as well. The little boy was expectantly looking up when the man said, "What are you looking at?"

The boy said, "There is one black balloon. Will that also go up if you cut it?"

"Son, it is not the colour, it is what is inside that makes it rise."

What is important is what is inside. It is not what is outside, not at all. When we come to Amma, she sees both the inside and the outside. If, like us, she sees only what is outside, how could she live the way she lives? Our character should be judged by what we manifest, not by what appears to be us. There is an expression: The clothes make the man. Obviously, that is rarely true. And one more thing: we should not judge the book by its cover.

Robin Hood lived an austere life in the woods and was a thief, but what was he doing? Taking from the rich and giving to the poor. On the other hand, there may be many people who are well-dressed, live in beautiful mansions, but are thieves or criminals. Looking outwardly respectable does not make one so. We shouldn't be deluded by the externals.

The Girl Who Loved Her Ring

Our whole life may play out without actually gaining any insight into the reality of people and situations, due to our taking the externals as a reflection of the internals. For example, many people seem to be deeply in love. But if the couple don't please each other, after sometime, their love decreases or even evaporates. Still worse, they may become enemies.

One lady was talking to her girlfriend, who said, "I heard you broke your engagement with Tom. What happened?"

"Oh, my feelings towards him changed, that's all."

"Well, are you going to return his engagement ring?"

"Oh no, my feelings towards the ring haven't changed!"

A Child's Love for His Parents

Sometimes kids are also like that. One day, a little boy went to school, but from the looks of him, he was very miserable. The teacher called him out, "Johnny, what is the matter?"

"I'm worried about something."

"What is the matter, Johnny, you're just a little boy?"

"It's my parents."

"What about your parents?"

"My dad works all day long. He wants to make sure I'm well clothed and well fed and sent to the best school in town. He is even working overtime to make sure that I get into a good college. And my mom, she cooks all day, cleans the house and looks after everything."

"So, when everything is fine, what are you worried about?"

Johnny replied, "I'm afraid they might try to escape!"

Don't be fooled by appearances. Everyone loves themselves the most. Try to understand what the Self truly is. Until the experience of our True Nature dawns, remember that we're living in the dream of Maya.

Patience & Discipline

"Children, spiritual life is possible only for one who has patience. It is not possible to measure one's spiritual growth only by seeing external actions. Spiritual advancement can be understood to a certain extent on the basis of one's reactions to adverse circumstances. How can a person who gets angry over a petty thing lead the world? Children, only a person with patience can guide others. Ego should be completely annihilated. No matter how many people sit in a chair, it doesn't complain. In the same way, regardless of how many people get angry with us, we should develop the strength to endure and forgive. Otherwise, there is no use in doing sadhana.

"Through anger, much of the power gained through sadhana will be lost. While a vehicle is running, not much energy is dissipated, but if we stop and start it again and again, more fuel will be spent. Likewise, getting angry drains power through every pore of the body. Though we may not see that the fuel is decreasing, when a cigarette lighter has been used ten or twenty times, its fuel will be spent. Similarly, the energy acquired through good thoughts can be lost in many ways. For instance, when we get angry, whatever we have gained through sadhana will be lost. When we talk, energy will be spent only through the mouth, but anger dissipates energy through the eyes and the ears as well as through every pore of the body."

Patience and Discipline

Amma touches upon some very important principles here, and these are not just spiritual principles but those that affect our everyday life. Why do we need patience? If we don't have patience, we may become a patient. And if we are very impatient, we may become an in-patient. So, patience is very important.

Sometimes, people come to Amma and want an immediate answer to their questions. Those who know her might have seen what she does. The more impatient a person is to get an answer, the more patient Amma is to not give the answer! She will just close her eyes as if nobody asked anything. Gradually, the impatience of the person decreases, and sometimes the answer dawns of its own accord.

The Buddha Teaches a Man to be Patient

One day, a man came to Lord Buddha with many questions. He was very impatient. He said, "I want to ask you many things and want a special darshan. You should answer all the things for me right now."

The Buddha said, "I'll answer every question you have, but only after one year. And for one year, you must keep your intellect, reasoning and doubts to yourself and do whatever I say. Be obedient and live with all of us here as a *bhikshu*, and after one year, you can ask me anything."

When the Buddha said this, there was another monk sitting under a tree who started loudly laughing. The other man thought, 'He is laughing at me. He is making fun of me.' So he went over, and said, "What is so funny?"

The monk said, "The same thing happened to me. If you have any questions, you'd better ask them now!"

The man went back after one year. The time was drawing near, but by that time, he had become very patient. His mind had become much more calm, and the questions had naturally dissolved. So what did he do? He started to avoid the Buddha. He felt a bit shy. Then the Buddha called him and said, "Okay, you can now bring back your intellect, your doubts and your questions and ask me anything you want." Naturally, he had nothing to ask. Everything was answered in the silence and patience he had gained.

This is one reason why Amma may not answer us. We may think, 'She doesn't even know the answer; that is why she is not answering me.' That is not the reason. The reason is, we should become patient. It is very important to become patient. Amma talks a lot about how the power gained through sadhana is lost, and the detrimental effects that impatience and anger have on our body, mind, and spiritual life.

The Body-Mind is Like a Computer

The body is somewhat like a computer, and the mind is somewhat like the programs that make the computer run, like hardware and software. One difference is that there is no warranty on the body. If it doesn't work, we can't trade it in. We have to adjust with what we've got. We can't upgrade it either, at least not until our next birth. And, just like a computer, it can be used in many different ways.

Some people are very artistic. They are programmed for art. It is the same with a computer; we can get a paint program and draw very beautiful pictures. Other people may be very business-minded; their software is business software. Similarly, we can get accounting programs or database programs. Some people are like children; they like to have fun all the time. They

Patience and Discipline

are programmed for having a good time, for having fun. For that, also, we can get computer games. But even though this computer of the body and mind can be used for many things, if there is a sudden surge or spark of electricity, then what happens? Just like an ordinary computer, it starts to act in a very strange, erratic way.

I had a funny experience like this once in Amritapuri. The electricity there used to be very erratic. It would go on and off all the time, and the voltage would wildly fluctuate. Air-conditioning that would work for any length of time was out of the question.

Those days were just the beginning of our using a computer in the ashram for typing and office work. We had only one computer. One day, I was typing something, and the voltage decreased. The air-conditioning went off, and the room started to get hotter and hotter. I wanted to take a break and was looking at the computer screen. It started to malfunction and type its own words. As it got hotter, 'zzzzzzzzz' appeared across the screen. I touched the keyboard and 'pppppppppp' came up on the screen. Whatever I tried, it wouldn't listen. I couldn't reason with it. Finally, I had to play God and pulled out the plug!

Similarly, our nervous system is very delicate. We don't realize it, especially when we're young, but anger and impatience take their toll on us. Gradually, our brain and nervous system get affected. They start to act in a strange way and don't obey us. We may inadvertently say the wrong thing and make a mess of things.

It is true that everybody gets angry, but anger has a very negative effect on our body. Everybody knows that whenever we feel tense or impatient or, when we are boiling with anger and explode, we feel very tired and exhausted afterwards. This is the physical effect. But what about the spiritual effect? That is what we're more concerned about here.

Amma says that impatience and anger drain our energy. For a spiritual person, reaching the spiritual goal is the most important thing. The goal is not just maintaining one's health. Health is not an eternal thing. Most of us who have come to Amma are serious about spiritual life. Some have reached a certain stage of spiritual evolution wherein we have realized that we don't want to be the slave of our mind anymore. We want to be able to control our mind. Most ordinary people do whatever their mind dictates. They never think about self-control. They may think, 'If we're lucky and have a good mind, everything is okay, and if we're unlucky and have a bad mind, then life is a mess.' But it shouldn't be up to the mind to determine our fate. We have free will, and we should be exercising it. That is one purpose of spiritual life and discipline.

To get hold of the mind and make it do as we like requires a lot of energy. The flow of the mind is very strong. Stopping it is like trying to cap an oil well that is on fire. It is always flowing out through the senses. It is always thinking and having feelings.

To get peace of mind and to become truly blissful, to have fruitful meditation, to experience ecstasy during devotional singing, we have to reach the source of the mind. That is where bliss comes from. There is no real happiness or bliss in anything of the world. It is within us. If we can uncover it, if we can make our mind still, it will reveal itself. Although the mind is getting dissipated all the time due to its extrovert nature, anger dissipates it more than anything else.

Anger Wastes the Energy Accumulated by Sadhana

Many people come to Amma and say, "I have been meditating twenty-five years and still not having any spiritual experience. What is the reason for this? I feel like God's grace will never come to me; God doesn't like me, Amma doesn't like me; God is partial." That is not the reason. The reason is that our sadhana is defective. Amma says we are like someone who works hard during the day, and then in the evening, buys peanuts with our money instead of some substantial food. In other words, our sadhana is hard earned, but we waste it on trivialities.

So, this is one reason we don't achieve much in spiritual life: there are so many leaks where our energy is going out, and one of the main ones is anger. We should not think that when we get angry, there is no effect afterwards. We have spent our money, our hard-earned spiritual sadhana at that time. We might have meditated in the morning for an hour, and all day long were doing our mantra and other spiritual practices. Then we got angry at someone and much of that spiritual wealth evaporated. We spent it and didn't get anything in return. We have to be careful, like a good plumber. Find the leaks and plug them!

Anger and impatience go hand in hand. First we become impatient, which culminates in anger. What is the root cause of impatience? Pride or ego. Amma says that the ego should be completely annihilated for good to result. How do we annihilate the ego? There are various ways.

Story of Eknath Taking a Bath

Eknath was a famous householder saint in Maharasthra during the 16th century . There was a jealous man in his village who hated him. Jealousy breeds hatred.

In the villages in India, many people take their daily bath in a nearby river. This is not only for maintaining cleanliness, but also for spiritual or religious purity. There was a river flowing by Eknath's village. Every morning, he would go there for his bath and then return home and do meditation, puja, and so on.

One day, the man who hated Eknath decided to express his hatred. He stood on the top of a building by the side of the road that Eknath was walking on. As Eknath was returning from his bath and came by the side of the building, the man, who was chewing betel nut and leaves (a kind of a digestive, dark red in colour) spit on him and it landed right on Eknath's head. What did Eknath do? What would we do in that situation? Shout at him? Punch him? No. He turned and went back to the river and took another bath. Then he came back again and what happened? This man spit on him again. Then what did he do? He turned and went and had another bath. Then again he came, and what happened? The man spit on him again. If nothing else, this man was very patient! This happened a hundred times, and each time, Eknath went and took a bath.

After a hundred times, seeing Eknath's patience, this man realized that Eknath was a saint.

Finally, the man thought, 'What a horrible thing I've done,' and ran downstairs and fell at Eknath's feet and said, "Please forgive me, please forgive me, I didn't realize what and who are."

Eknath said, "What's the matter? You didn't do anything."

The man said, "No, no. I've been spitting on you all morning."

Eknath said, "No, I should thank you, because usually, I have a bath once a day in the holy river. Today, I had a hundred baths. There is nothing that I can do for you in return for the great grace that you've given to me. At least let me touch your feet." He prostrated to this man.

This is a true story. We can develop patience by thinking of the great patient ones, the mahatmas. Whenever we have an opportunity to be patient, just think of that incident. How did Eknath act under such provocation? After all, nobody is beating us up or spitting in our face. Somebody may just do something to us that we don't like, or somebody may not cooperate with us, or somebody may be doing something too slowly, or somebody may insult us. We should try to mould our life, our reactions, to be in line with those of the mahatmas. We have so many examples in Amma's life also. If we read her life story, we can find them.

Buddha Gets Abused and Keeps Quiet

There is another way. Just remain indifferent in these provocative situations; be detached.

Somebody came to the Buddha and started abusing him, saying many mean things to him. What do you think Buddha did? He sat calmly. He just sat there and listened. Then he turned to the man and said, "I want to ask you something. Suppose you cook a big feast of delicious food for some guests, and the guests never come. What would you do?"

"I'd eat all the food myself."

Buddha said, "That is exactly the point. You served me all this delicious abuse, but I'm not going to eat it, so you're going to have to eat it yourself." Buddha didn't get upset. He was indifferent, detached. Only the abuser had to suffer with a restless mind. Let anybody say anything to us; just remain detached. Remember Buddha and act like him. That is one way of doing it.

Amma says,

> "Someone may disagree with you and another may argue with you. Don't react. Try to be calm. Your calmness will disarm the other person. If you have any complaints, come and tell Amma about it, but don't get angry. Don't speak roughly or use harsh words."

Amma's Advice on How to Stop Anger

Amma says to come and tell her about it. Suppose we're in our office and somebody gets angry with us. Should we get on the next plane to India and go to Amritapuri and tell Amma about what that person said? Obviously not. Then what to do? Tell Amma about it in your mind. This is what Amma means. That will dissipate the energy, the reaction that is coming up. Tell her, "Amma, see how that man is treating me. Doesn't he know that I'm your devotee?"

> "If anger arises in you, do not express it immediately. Leave the place, go sit somewhere by yourself, and contemplate, meditate. You'll find that the cause of your anger is not in the other person, but within you. It is not the other person that causes it, but your own past. The past is your reference book. Anger is within you, and someone accidentally touches the anger in you and you erupt."

The Professor Who Wrote to His Student

A professor gave a talk on a radio show about a subject that he didn't really know very well. The next day, he received a letter from a lady that was very abusive. She wrote, "If you don't know what you're talking about, what are you doing on a radio show?"

This man thought that he was an authority on his subject. He was a well-known professor, so his ego felt pricked. He got very angry. He took out a pen and paper and wrote a scathing reply. He put it in an envelop, sealed it, and was going to mail it, when he realized the post office was closed, so he just left it on his desk.

The next morning when he came in and saw the letter on his desk, he thought, 'Let me just read it and see what I wrote before I send it.' So, he read it and thought, 'Oh my, I was very impulsive and harsh with this lady. After all, she didn't say that bad of a thing to me.' So he rewrote it and sealed it. But then he thought, 'If twelve hours of waiting made my mind change so much, maybe I should wait another twelve hours before I mail this letter.'

So, he kept it in the drawer, and after twelve hours, pulled it out and read it again. He thought, 'This is still not a very good letter. It's kind of nasty.' So, he wrote it again and then again. Unknowingly, he followed the advice to wait, to leave the place, and to not express anger immediately. Finally he wrote, "Dear Madam, I'm so grateful to you for having pointed out my mistakes. I'd like to meet you. Maybe we could go out for dinner." Wow! What a difference.

Slowly, the anger will decrease, and then we'll see that it wasn't the person or the situation that was making us angry; it was our own past habit of getting angry, that is all. We have gotten angry before, and we have a subtle remembrance of the pleasure of expressing our anger. So, when the opportunity comes again and somebody touches a 'tender' place, then that remembrance of how satisfying it was to get angry pops up and again we get angry. Amma says that we have to stop that chain reaction sometime or other, the sooner the better. Even though we may not be able to feel calm at that moment, at least just stop and go somewhere else. Let it cool down. That will be the beginning of the end of the anger.

> "Anger is like an infected wound; when somebody touches it, you feel pain, and if the touch is hard, pus and blood will come out creating more pain. Yes, anger is a deep wound; it is a disease that needs to be treated; it needs your compassion and your loving attention."

Attention, that is what many of us are lacking. We've got some negativity problems, but we don't pay any attention to them. We sort of push them under the rug until we leave the Earth. They need our attention.

> "Therefore, when someone gets angry, remember that he is a sick person. Don't make him more sick. Don't let more blood flow out of his wound. Don't make him experience more pain by pressing and squeezing harder and harder."

We should keep aside our own anger. When someone else is getting angry, don't make it worse by provoking him. Just as we feel a lot of pain after getting angry, the other person also feels so. Don't squeeze the poor person. Take pity on him.

> "An angry person needs comforting. Soothe his wounds. Children, Amma wants to remind you that it is an opportunity to develop your love. None of you are Self-realized. Therefore, disagreements can happen, but try to practice love and patience."

Another way that the ego expresses itself and loses energy is to find fault with everybody and everything except itself. It thinks, 'I'm okay. Nobody else is. They're all at fault. They all have so many faults, but I'm alright.' Then they get angry at people and criticize them and lose their energy.

The Story of Seeing God in Everyone

There was a great yogi sitting in the Himalayas in deep samadhi. His mind was perfectly still. One day, the head of a distant monastery made a long journey to see this mahatma and arrived there. His monastery used to be great and many people joined there. There was even a waiting list to join. On the weekends, many visitors would come, and the meditation hall was always full; the chanting was sublime. However, gradually, things got worse and worse. People didn't want to join anymore. The meditation hall became empty; nobody was chanting. Finally, there was just a skeleton crew left; a few old monks remained. They used to somehow keep everything going, but even they were miserable.

The head of the monastery was at his wits' end to figure out what could fix the situation. He heard about this great mahatma in the Himalayas, and thought the mahatma could help him. Approaching the mahatma, he did his *pranam* and stood there. The mahatma opened his eyes and looked at him.

"What do you want? Why have you come here?"

The monk said, "Our monastery has become lifeless. No one wants to stay there anymore. Are we doing something wrong?"

"Yes. You're doing something wrong, albeit out of ignorance."

"Really, what is it?"

"You are ignorant of the fact that one of the people living in your monastery is an avatar, an incarnation of God, a messiah. Because of that ignorance, because of mistreating him, all these problems have come."

The monk was wonderstruck.

"There is an avatar in our monastery? Wait until I go back and tell everybody."

So, he ran back to the monastery, called all the monks together, and said, "That mahatma in the Himalayas said that one of us is an avatar, a messiah; he is in disguise."

They said, "We can't believe it. What are you talking about? It couldn't be the cook; he doesn't even know how to cook. It couldn't be the secretary; he makes so many grammatical mistakes, he's a mess. It certainly isn't the accountant; we're losing money every day. In fact, everybody here is full of faults. None of us could be the avatar."

The monk said, "No. That mahatma couldn't be wrong. He said one of us is an avatar and that he is in disguise. So it is better we treat everybody with respect and reverence, because we don't know which one he is. He is in disguise and he is not going to tell us."

After that, everybody treated everybody else with respect, devotion and reverence. The whole atmosphere changed. And, pretty soon, there was a waiting list to get in. People wanted to join the monastery. The meditation hall became full. There was great chanting, and it was a glorious monastery once again.

This is how we can get rid of the ego. Consider that each one is God. Or, if we can't do that, try to remember the look in Amma's eyes when she looks at us and at every person that comes to her. What is that look? What is she seeing? Is she seeing us as an individual? No. She is seeing the Common Denominator, the thing that is the same in everybody. That is God, the Light of Consciousness. Try to develop that attitude and then the ego will decrease. The impatience will get less, the anger will subside, and then the mind will become peaceful. Then our meditation will be successful. We will experience ecstasy and become blissful children of the Divine Mother!

Persistence & Devotion

"Children, keeping a strict timetable is what is necessary for a spiritual aspirant. There should be a daily routine of japa and meditation at the same time and for a set duration. The habit of meditating every day at a fixed time should be developed. This habit will guide us. Those who have a regular timetable of spiritual discipline will automatically follow it at the fixed time. One who has grown accustomed to drinking tea at a particular time must get tea at that time. Otherwise he will become restless and run for tea."

Every week we're really talking about the same thing in various packages. It is about the goal of human life, which, according to Amma and so many sages and religions, is to know our Self. Self-realization is the real purpose of spiritual life. Just going to temples and praying to God and reading books is not all there is to spiritual life. Real spiritual life is to know our Self; not what we feel is ourself, the body and the changing personality, but the real Self, the real 'I' in us. Or, from the viewpoint of devotion, to attain oneness with our Source, with the Creator, with God. Only that will give us the satisfaction that we're seeking.

Real spiritual life teaches us how to attain lasting peace of mind and become truly happy. That implies avoiding actions that are going to cause future sorrow and engaging in actions that are going to make us happy. For that, we have to learn the teachings of the sages and the scriptures.

In essence, all scriptures and sages, and that includes Amma, say the same thing: To achieve peace of mind, we must tame the mind and the senses. This is the teaching of the *Bhagavad Gita*. To do this, a certain amount of systematic discipline is necessary. There are no shortcuts, and if we can achieve that equipoise—equal-mindedness in pleasure and pain, heat and cold, amongst this world of opposites—then indescribable bliss will start to bubble up from within. We'll start to experience an inner bliss that we never had an inkling of. Then, the reality of the Self, the reality of God's Presence, will become clearer and clearer as time passes and we continue doing our sadhana. Until then, it is just a matter of faith in believing the words of the scriptures and the sages. Or, we might have been fortunate enough to get a glimpse of something like that either through our *punyam* (past meritorious actions), or through the association with someone like Amma.

The mind is a bundle of habits. These are called *vasanas*. They can be positive and helpful for us to reach this goal. They can also be negative and take us away from it. When we remember what our goal is and always keep it in mind, our path will become clear and understandable.

We have to create strong spiritual habits which will awaken us from this slumber of life and death and which will give us peace of mind, enabling us to tame our mind. It is no mysterious thing. It is a scientific method, and it can become our second nature. Right now, our mind may be so distracted and so outward bent that its nature is to never think about God or about the Self or Guru. But through regular discipline, a daily routine, a timetable, it can become such that one never thinks about anything other than God. There will be a constant flow of the consciousness or mind towards God.

The Habitual Nature of the Mind

The habitual nature of the mind can get us into trouble. Once, a person found a book in a used bookstore. When he took it home, he looked at the back of the book and saw some writing. It said, "On the shore of the sea, in a certain place, there is a philosopher's stone." A philosopher's stone is a stone that turns whatever it touches into gold. It may be a myth, but in many ancient cultures, such a thing was said to exist. So, "By the sea, in a certain place, there are numerous black stones, and they all look similar, but one of them is the philosopher's stone." How is one to find out which stone it is? "And they all look similar, but the difference is that the philosopher's stone is warm, as if it is alive, and all the other stones are cool to the touch."

This man thought, 'This is a very old book, and in those days, people didn't play practical jokes. So this must be the truth.' He borrowed money enough to stay for a year by the seaside and went to the place and found where all these stones were. He would pick up one, and if it felt cold, would throw it far into the sea.

This went on day after day, month after month, until a year had passed, but he still hadn't found it. So he borrowed some more money and stayed there for another two years. After three years of doing like this, one day, he picked up a stone that felt warm, but without thinking, he automatically threw it into the sea!

This is the nature of habit. This is the nature of the mind. However, we can use this quality to train it in such a way that it will automatically cling to the thought of God or a mantra all the time.

Mind's Impulsive Nature

The mind also has an impulsive nature. In the Mahabharata epic, there is a story about this. The Pandava brothers were wandering in exile in the forest. They were very thirsty, so they sent one of the brothers, Nakula, to find water to drink. He came across a beautiful lake and was about to have a drink, when he heard a voice coming from the trees. It said, "Who are you? This is my lake, and if you don't first answer my questions, you'll die. Don't drink! You may drink only after answering my questions."

The Pandavas were kings, and so they were proud. Nakula said, "Ha, who are you? I'll drink if I want to!" Impulsiveness asserted itself. As soon as he drank the water, he fell down dead!

One after another, the brothers came in search of the missing brother and the water, and the same thing happened. Each one said, "Who do you think you are? I can drink the water if I want," and each one drank and died on the spot.

However, the last one, Yudhisthira, was the spiritual one. He was born with a spiritual nature. What did he do? When he heard the voice, he controlled his impulsive nature. That is what a real spiritual person will do. They may react a little, but immediately they will stop and proceed with caution. This is what Yudhisthira did. He might have felt a little bit like, 'Who is this?' But he saw the situation; all his brothers were lying there, dead by the side of the lake. He thought, 'There must be some truth in these words.' See, the other four were impulsive; even though they saw the dead bodies, they didn't care to listen. That is the power of impulse.

Then he answered the questions and was given permission to drink. It is a long story, but he was given a boon to revive the other brothers and they all came back to life. Everybody lived happily ever after…sort of. The Mahabharata is a tragedy, so they didn't exactly live happily ever after.

This is how a bad habit can get us in trouble. However, we can use this habitual nature of the mind to follow a strict timetable, do japa and meditation at the same time, for the same length of time, every single day.

The Delaying Mind

The mind has got another tricky side—to avoid purification. It thinks, 'I'll do it, but not today, maybe tomorrow. After all, what's the hurry?' We may have a bad habit that we're trying to stop, but we'll think, 'Not today. It will be easier tomorrow.' Unfortunately, tomorrow also becomes tomorrow and so on.

One day, a priest was walking down the road and noticed a group of his parishioners in a nearby building. And where were they? In a bar! So he was very upset. He walked in there and scolded them,"Come on, let's go!"

He herded all of them to the church and said, "This is terrible. What is the use of my teaching you every Sunday? All right, everybody who wants to go to Heaven, stand on the left side of the room." Immediately, everybody moved to the left side except one man.

The priest said,"Don't you want to go to Heaven?"

"No."

"What? I can't believe it. You don't want to go to Heaven when you die?"

"Of course I want to go to Heaven when I die. I thought you meant right now!"

We're willing to do good things, but not right now. That is the problem.

Importance of Regularly Using An Alarm Clock

So how to develop good habits? Actually, once we start, it becomes quite natural. For example, yogis tell us to get up at four o'clock in the morning; that is the best time for spiritual practice. So we should set our alarm clock for four o'clock. The first couple days, even weeks, maybe months for some of us, it will be very hard to get up and stay up. Some people even use two alarm clocks to get up; one set to 3:50 am and the other for 4 am. If we do this everyday without fail, eventually, we won't need an alarm clock. An inner alarm will wake us just before 4 am. It takes some days to start to happen, but once it is established, it will continue for years. After that, it is very difficult to give it up even if we want to. If we miss a day, whether it is getting up at the right time, or doing japa or some other practice, we'll start to feel uneasy. We will feel out of whack the whole day. This is what Amma is saying, that we will feel like a person who doesn't get his tea at the right time and becomes restless. In the same way, if we do regular spiritual practices, we will start to experience some peace and pleasure from that, and if we miss it even one day, we'll feel very bad. This is because our mind and body start to vibrate at a purer frequency due to our sadhana. If we neglect it, a feeling of disharmony happens, and we feel as if there is something wrong.

I used to get up at three-thirty every morning. Whatever time I would go to sleep (and it was usually late, eleven or twelve at night), I would still get up at three-thirty. Three-thirty means exactly three-thirty. One day, I woke up at three-thirty-one. The alarm went off at three-thirty. I rolled over, and said to myself, 'I'll get up in a moment,' but sometimes that moment will become an hour or two. This time, the moment became a minute. It was three-thirty one. The whole day was a mess. Every single thing was one minute late, until I went to sleep. I didn't get any peace of mind that whole day, because this one minute was out of synch.

We can do it. It is not impossible. Then, if we meditate every day and do our spiritual practices regularly, we can judge clearly whether we are making progress or are going backwards. I asked myself, 'What caused this distraction today? What was different from yesterday? Yesterday, I had good meditation. Today, I'm not having good meditation.' If we're very regular, we'll be able to find the causes for the obstacles coming up, for going backwards, for the digressions.

Don't think that repetition is a small thing. Repetition is the key to Self-realization. For example: take mantra japa. We don't even have to know the meaning of our mantra. That is what Amma says. "It is enough if you just repeat it." Just practice the mantra, again and again and again. Gradually, it will purify the mind. It will decrease the thoughts, and show the way to proceed.

The Swami Who Chanted Ramayana 108 Times

I once knew a swami who had been told by a mahatma to read the *Tulasi Ramayana* one hundred and eight times. *Tulasi Ramayana* is not a small book; it contains nearly 11,000 verses. It is a wonderful book; it is divine. It is the story of Lord Rama's incarnation, written by a mahatma named Tulasidas. It is exquisite.

The swami took it to heart. He thought, 'If a mahatma tells me to do a thing, God is telling me to do that thing.' That is how we should interact with great souls. If they tell us to do a thing, don't take it lightly, as if somebody on the street has told to you to do something. Take it that God Himself/Herself has told you to do that. So, he took it and started sitting and reading. What was he doing at other times? He wasn't doing anything at other times. He spent almost eighteen hours of the day reading *Tulasi Ramayana* and the other six hours sleeping, eating, bathing and so on.

He told me that when he reached the hundredth repetition, "Up to that point, it was extremely difficult. Sometimes I'd fall asleep on top of the book, or I'd feel very bored or fed up. I'd think to myself, 'How am I going to get through this? This is impossible. I was foolish to accept this kind of discipline.'" Even then, he persisted. He used to get up and walk around the book, or walk around the room.

But he decided that he was somehow going to do this, that there must be something in it. By the hundred and first repetition, the inner meaning of Tulasidas' words were flashing on his mind, and waves of bliss were drowning him in ecstasy. He couldn't read even one line without bursting into tears. He'd lose all consciousness of the world. Only the Presence of God would shine in his mind.

Repetition Brings Grace

This had nothing to do with intellectually understanding the text. Some people want to understand the inner meaning of the scriptures like *Srimad Bhagavata, Mahabharata* or the *Ramayana*. They look for books or people who can explain these things. For example, they may be told that the inner meaning of Lord Krishna's life is the story of the individual soul's or *jiva's* pilgrimage back to God. The gopis are the nerves in the body and Krishna is the Paramatman or consciousness flowing through those nerves. When the gopis went up to the seventh floor of a building to see Krishna as He was walking down the road, the meaning is about the *kundalini shakti* going up to the *sahasrara chakra* in the top of the head and experiencing union with God. The throwing down of flowers on Him represents the resultant shower of Divine Bliss. This may be true, but the use of this information, spiritually speaking, is limited.

Some intellectually inclined people will always think, "What is the meaning of this story?" But we don't have to understand the inner meaning of a story or the meaning of a mantra to experience its power. If we read a book again and again that was written by a mahatma like Tulasidas or any text that was composed by a rishi or sage like Vyasa, what finally happens? The grace or blessings of that mahatma or rishi start to manifest in us despite who or what we are intellectually, and then our heart blossoms in bliss, insight, ecstasy, and intuition. There is no other way for this to happen. Intellectual knowledge will not bring it about. We must get it only through grace, and grace is gotten through repetition and discipline. There is no other way.

The Shankaracharya of Puri

During the mid-1950's, there was a scholarly brahmin who was to become the Shankaracharya of Puri. He was a Vedic scholar and found some strange mantras occurring in various places in the *Atharva Veda* during his studies. They did not seem to make any sense. They were in the form of mysterious mathematical formulas such as, "By one more than the previous one." He thought, 'What did the ancient sages mean when they were writing this?' He couldn't understand it, but he had the faith that whatever the ancient rishis said must be true.

So he went to a mahatma who was staying in a holy place called Sringeri and asked, "What is the meaning of this?"

The mahatma said, "I can't tell you that, but I'll tell you how to find out. I'll give you a place to stay in the woods near the ashram, and you should engage in repeating Goddess Saraswati's mantra while continuing your studies. As She is the deity presiding over knowledge and learning, She may reveal the meaning of the mantras if She is pleased with your tapas."

For eight years, most of his days and nights were spent repeating the mantra to get the grace of Saraswati. Eventually, the meaning of the Vedic mantras started to dawn on him; they flashed on his mind. The mantras were mathematical formulas. Once their application was understood, any mathematical problem could be done in one step! He then wrote a book entitled *Vedic Mathematics*, which contains a summary of his revelation. This is another example of grace through repetition. Later, he was invited to America and taught this system in many of the universities; people were amazed.

I told one of Amma's devotees about this book. He bought a copy, took it to the Los Alamos Nuclear Research Center in New Mexico, and showed it to some of the scientists there; they couldn't believe it, because that system had never been seen before, and nobody could have ever figured it out using only their intellect.

We should not think that developing good habits and repetition of spiritual practices are a lot of nonsense. If Amma says to regularly to repeat our mantra or regularly do our meditation, she is serious about it; not just to get a good habit. It is a way to get grace, and we can't get grace in any other way. We have to develop discipline and good habits. Don't feel discouraged hearing about people that did such seemingly super-human feats. It is true that we can't even imagine sitting in a hut for eight years repeating one mantra, or reading a book one hundred and eight times for twenty hours a day. Yet we can do what we can. Gradually, our strength will increase, and we also will do great things.

Abraham Lincoln: An Image of Persistence

At the beginning of the 19th century, there was a very unsuccessful person who lived in America. He was probably one of the most unsuccessful people that ever lived. However, we would be surprised to hear that person was Abraham Lincoln! He is considered to be one of the great people in American history. I'd just like to read to you what he went through, a sort of chronology of

Persistence and Devotion

his life. I found it very interesting because he was known for his persistence, and if an ordinary person can persist like that and succeed, anybody can.

In 1816, his family was forced out of their home, and he had to work to support them. In 1818, his mother died. In 1831, he failed in business. In 1832, he ran for the state legislature and lost. In 1832, he also lost his job. He wanted to go to law school, but the school board would not give him admission. In 1833, he borrowed some money from a friend to begin a business, and by the end of the year, he was bankrupt. He spent the next seventeen years of his life paying off this debt. In 1834, he ran for the state legislature again and won. In 1835, he was engaged to be married, but his sweetheart died. In 1836, he had a total nervous breakdown, and was in bed for six months. In 1838, he sought to become Speaker of the State Legislature and was defeated. He sought to become an elector and was defeated. He ran for Congress and lost. Two years later, he ran for Congress again and won. In 1848, he ran for re-election to Congress and lost. Then he sought a job as a land officer in his home state and was rejected. He ran for the Senate and lost. He sought the vice-presidential nomination and lost, and he ran for the Senate again in 1858 and lost again. Finally, two years after that, he was elected President of the United States!

He was just an ordinary person with ordinary desires and ordinary ambitions, but what persistence! We could say ninety-five percent of his life was spent meeting with failure, frustration and obstacles. He didn't give up, and he achieved the highest worldly position in the country. We're aiming for far higher than that, so how much more persistence we should have?

Greatness of Humility

> "Huge trees will be uprooted and buildings will collapse in a cyclone, but no matter how strong a cyclone is, it cannot affect the grass. This is the greatness of humility. To bow down to others is not weakness; we should have the greatness to bow down even to the grass. If a person decides to take a bath, but is not ready to bow down to the river, his body will remain dirty. A sadhak, by saying that he will not bow down to others, is not allowing his ignorance to be destroyed."
>
> —*Amma*

This is not only about the act of physically bowing down as a sign of humility, but more importantly, about the need of a sadhak being humble. Most people want to be in a position of superiority. This tendency is an obstruction to leading a spiritual life. Pride is a sign of spiritual ignorance.

When I was living in Tiruvannamalai, there were two mahatmas staying there. A couple, a husband and wife visiting from America, came with me one day to visit them. Some devotees had also come from Madras. As the devotees came in, they bowed down to the mahatmas as a sign of respect and humility. The American couple had no knowledge of any of the traditional ways of India, so when these devotees got up and left the room, they turned to the swamis and said, "Why do they demean themselves like that before you, and why do you accept it?"

One swami turned to the man and said, "Tell me one thing. When you want to get a promotion, don't you bow down to your boss?"

"Of course not. I don't bow down like this before anybody."

"Maybe not like this, but in every other way except physically, you are bowing down to your boss to get his favour. Surely your body language and speech will show that. These people also want a promotion, a spiritual promotion, and they feel we can give them that. They're showing their humility before us in this way so that their intentions are obvious, and that they are ready to be receptive to our advice."

Amma continues,

> "Man egotistically claims that by a mere pressing of a button, the world can be burnt to ashes. To press the button, the hand must move. He doesn't think about the power behind this movement. Man says that he has conquered the world. He does not even have the capacity to count the grains of sand under his own feet. Such small fries say they have conquered the world.
>
> "Suppose a man gets angry with you for no reason. Even at that time, a sadhak should have the attitude to bow down to him, realizing that it is a play of God to test him. Only then can it be said that the benefit of meditation has been attained. Children, even when a man is cutting a tree down from its very root, it gives him shade. A spiritual aspirant should also be like this. Only he who prays, even for the welfare of those who torment him, can become a truly spiritual person."

Everybody, whoever they are, be they the lowest of beings, still feels they are greater than others. This is called *abhimanam* or false pride. Yet if we look around, we will realize that we're nothing. Any moment anything can happen to us. If our heart stops, we're finished. For all our so-called greatness, what we call our self is ultimately a dead body. What is really great in this world is death.

Nobody can stand before that. Death is the Great Leveller. All those that claimed that they would not die are gone.

One day, I was sitting in a bus waiting to go somewhere. The girl sitting in the seat in front of me was saying goodbye to her father, who was standing by her window outside. Suddenly, he collapsed and died! I felt God was showing me the truth of life, that death is always present. What is there to be proud about?

This is what Amma is saying, that pride is born of ignorance. We don't think; we don't see the truth of things, so we become proud. And pride separates us from our real Self, from God. We have some energy, we have some intelligence, we have a small reservoir of these things, but they can dry up in a moment. Whatever little intelligence we have, whatever little strength we have, we should understand that it is not ours; it belongs to the Creator. This is what Amma is saying, that the power in the hand is not yours; it belongs to the Source.

Story From Kenopanishad

In the *Upanishads*, there is a very well known story about this. It is in the *Kenopanishad*. "*Keno*" means, "to whom?" To whom does everything belong?

As usual, the gods and the demons had a big fight. The gods won the fight and became very proud, thinking that all the glory was theirs, that all the greatness was theirs. However, God doesn't like His devotees to be proud, so the formless Being took a form and came to the gods to teach them a lesson.

On seeing this strange looking Being, Agni, the god of fire, was chosen to find out who it was. He said, "Who are you?" Not even, "Excuse me, hello," just, "Who are you?"

The Being said, "Who are you?"

Agni said, "I'm the god of fire."

"Ah, are you powerful?"

"Am I powerful? I can burn up this whole world, this whole universe. I can burn it up just like that!"

"Ha! Okay, can you burn up this piece of straw?" And he put a piece of straw in front of Agni. Agni pounced on it; he was burning with all his might, like a star with millions of degrees of heat, but the straw just sat there, cool as a cucumber. Nothing happened. Agni felt a little bit humbled. You can imagine, he couldn't even make a straw catch fire!

So he went back with his head hanging down and told the other gods, "I don't know who that is, but I couldn't burn even his piece of straw."

"Okay, let Vayu, the god of wind, find out who it is." So the wind god went there and said, "Who are you?"

"We'll see about that later. Who are you?"

"I am Vayu, the god of wind."

"Are you powerful?"

"Am I powerful? You never heard of me? Nothing can stand before me. I can blow away anything in this whole universe. Cyclones, tornadoes, hurricanes—those are just a little breath from my nostrils."

"Oh, okay. Here is a straw; blow away this piece of straw and I'll believe you."

Vayu jumped on it. He was huffing and puffing. There was a five hundred mile an hour hurricane, but the straw wasn't budging. He became really upset and went back, and told the other gods, "I don't know who this Being is."

Indra, the king of the gods, saw what was going on and suspected that this Being actually was God. Who else could it be? Indra's mind was different from the other gods' minds. He was humble. We may bow down to God, but we may be full of pride inwardly. On the other hand, we may not show our humility outwardly, but if the inner feeling is there, God immediately knows. Even though king of the gods, Indra had inner humility. He thought, 'Uh oh, it must be God.'

So he went to see Him, but before he could reach the place, the Being disappeared, and who was there in his place? The Divine Mother, the Goddess of Wisdom. He bowed down to Her and said, "Mother, who was that?" She replied, "That was Brahman. That was the Absolute Being from whom we get all our power. Don't think that your power is your own." This is the lesson that they learned. This is what Amma is saying, that by ourselves, we're nothing, we're nobody. Whatever little power that we have is from God.

Familiarity With Saints May Breed Contempt

Sometimes, out of pride and ignorance, we think that we are equal or greater than our Guru or a saint. Many people come to Amma, become familiar with her, and then start to look at her with critical eyes, instead of with love and respect, devotion and faith. They start to criticize, 'If Amma is divine, why does she act like that? Why does she say things like that? Since she is divine, she shouldn't eat, she shouldn't sleep, she shouldn't breathe. She should walk above the ground. She should levitate.' This is how some people think.

Their love and devotion evaporate and instead, doubts and criticisms start to pop up. What are their source? Pride and one's own fault-finding mind. Nevertheless, Amma doesn't get angry. She finds some way or other to bring around the devotee, so that their faith gets completely established and they get full devotion and grace as a result.

Story of Garuda and Kakabhushundi

There is a story in the *Tulasi Ramayana* about two devotees for whom this happened. Even though we are going to talk about Lord Rama, just substitute Amma instead.

During the war, when Rama was fighting with the demon king, Ravana, there was an instance when Ravana's son, Indrajit, shot two arrows, one at Rama, and one at Rama's brother, Lakshmana. These arrows turned into snakes, which became rope-like and were called *nagapasas*. They wrapped around Rama and Lakshmana, who became unconscious and were lying there completely corpse-like.

The eagle, Garuda, Lord Vishnu's mount, saw this and thought, 'What is this? Rama is an avatar. He is the incarnation of Lord Vishnu and is my Lord, but He is lying there, dead as a doornail. I don't understand. Maybe He is not God. Maybe I made a mistake. All these years I've been flying Him around, and I'm even more powerful than Him. Those snakes couldn't have done anything to me; I would have eaten them.' This is how the devotee's mind may start to work.

After some time, Rama revived, and everything was okay. However, because of his perverted thought, Garuda became more and more confused and restless, and everything started to fall apart for him. Eventually, he couldn't function properly and became completely miserable.

This is how the mind is. Just think one bad thought, one really *adharmic* thought. We may totally forget about it. Nevertheless, the downward fall begins from that moment onwards. We become miserable but don't have the slightest idea where it all started. Some people say, "I'm so sad but I don't know why. Everything seems to be all right, but I'm miserable." Maybe this is why. It all started with a seemingly harmless negative thought that we did not give any importance to. However, if God's or Guru's grace is there for us, we'll figure it out, eventually.

Garuda couldn't figure it out. What did he do? He went to Lord Siva. Since he is a divine bird, he can go anywhere he wants. So he went to Lord Siva and said, "I don't know what is wrong with me. I'm so confused."

Lord Siva said, "I can tell you what is wrong; you made a mistake. You thought that Rama was an ordinary person and that you are so great. Let me tell you, I know how you can become okay. Go to the Himalayas, and a bird is there whose name is Kakabhushundi. Find him, and he'll make everything all right for you."

This was a big step down for Garuda. Garuda is a big eagle. He is the most powerful bird in creation. Kakabhushundi is just a little crow. Now he had to go to see this crow and humble himself.

So he went to the Himalayas and saw Kakabhushundi who got up and said, "Oh please, Maharaj, come and sit on the throne," and he worshipped Garuda. We must remember that Garuda is the king of the birds.

Garuda said, "I've got a problem. Lord Siva said that you can solve it. Tell me what I am to do."

The crow said, "You know, I had the same problem."

"Really? What happened to you?"

"During every cycle of creation, Rama takes birth into this world, and I also go to see Him when He is a child. I love to see the *bala lilas*, the antics of when He was a child. I am very, very old. I've been doing this since millions of years, and the last time that I did it, a real problem arose."

Garuda said, "Really? What was it?"

Kakabhushundi said, "Well, I was flying around in the court and pecking at Rama and watching Him. He was dancing around like a little baby and started crying. He tried to catch me with His hands and pulled out some of my feathers, and then started screaming for His mother Kausalya. I thought, 'What is going on here? This is the Lord of the Universe? He is acting in such a silly way. Is this really Lord Vishnu?' And as soon as I had that thought, all the trouble started. He caught me and put me in His mouth and swallowed me!

"It seemed as if a hundred cycles had been spent in my wanderings through many universes. At last, after all my travels, I came to my own hermitage and stayed there for sometime. Meanwhile, as I happened to hear of my Lord's birth in Ayodhya, I started up and ran in an overwhelming ecstasy of love, and went to witness the grand festival of Rama's birth, as I have already told you.

"It need hardly be said that all this happened inside the belly of my Lord. Thus, in the belly of Sri Rama, I beheld several universes. But what I saw could only be seen with one's eyes. It was beyond all telling. There again, I beheld the divine Sri Rama, the Lord of Maya. I pondered again and again, but my understanding was obscured by the mists of delusion. In less than an hour, I had seen everything."

Kakabhushundi felt as if he had been in there for hundreds of years, seeing all those universes, but actually it only took one hour.

"My soul being utterly bewildered, I was lost in a maze. Seeing my distress, the gracious Lord laughed, and the moment He laughed, I came out of His mouth.

"Rama again began the same childlike pranks with me, and I reasoned with myself in every way I could, but my mind knew no peace. Seeing this childlike play, and recalling that glory which I had just seen inside His belly, I lost consciousness of my body, and crying, 'Save me, save me, O Rama,' I dropped to the ground. No other word came out of my mouth. When the Lord saw me overpowered with love and humility, He immediately checked the power of His Maya.

"The Lord who is so merciful to the afflicted, placed His lotus hand on my head, and relieved me of all sorrows. The gracious Sri Rama rid me of my deep-rooted error. As I reflected on His glory, my mind was flooded with joy. Seeing the Lord's loving kindness to His devotees, my heart began to throb with love. With eyes full of tears and joining my palms, and every hair of my body standing on end, I then made my supplication to Him in many ways. Hearing my loving words, and seeing the wretched plight of His servant, Sri Rama spoke in words that were not only soft and pleasing, yet profound at the same time.

"'Kakabhushundi, ask of Me a boon, knowing Me to be highly pleased with you. Be it mystic powers, fabulous wealth, or liberation—which is the fount of all joy – or spiritual wisdom, critical judgment, dispassion, realization, and numerous other virtues, which cannot be easily attained in this world even by sages today; I am prepared to give you all, undoubtedly.'"

It wasn't enough that Kakabhushundi suffered inside Rama's belly for so long. Now he also was being tempted. If we were in his place, what would we ask for? Think it over.

"On hearing the words of the Lord, I was overwhelmed with love, and began to reason thus within myself. 'The Lord, it is true, has promised to give me all kinds of blessings, but He didn't offer to grant me devotion to His feet. Without such devotion, all sorts of virtues and blessings are like so many dishes without salt. Of what avail is any blessing without devotion?'

"Pondering thus, I replied, 'If it is Your pleasure, my Lord, to grant me a boon, and if You are kind and affectionate to me, I ask You my cherished boon, O Master, for You are generous and know the secrets of all hearts. O Lord, Sri Rama, Tree of Paradise to the devotees, Friend of the supplicant, Ocean of Compassion, Abode of Bliss; in Your mercy, grant me that devotion to Your feet, uninterrupted and unalloyed, that the Vedas and the Puranas extol, which is sought after by the sages and the great yogis but attained by few, and that, too, only by the Lord's grace."

"'So be it', said Rama. 'Listen, Kakabhushundi, you have sound judgment, and it is no wonder, therefore, that you want this boon. No one in this world is as highly blessed as you, since you have sought the gift of devotion, which is the fountain of all blessings, and which even sages cannot obtain, despite all their efforts, even though they consume their body in the fire of prayer and meditation. I am pleased to see your judgment in that you have sought devotion, which is extremely dear to My heart. Listen, by My grace, all good qualities shall abide in your heart— devotion, spiritual wisdom, realization, dispassion, yoga, and My exploits as well as their secrets, and by My grace you shall obtain insight into all these and shall not be required to undergo the rigours of sadhana.'"

It would seem that, if we get devotion, then we don't even have to do sadhana! Let's see what tonight's bhajan is going to be like! Seriously, we shouldn't forget that, to get devotion, we do have to do a lot of sadhana and eventually renounce even the ego of 'doing sadhana.'

"'None of the errors that arise from Maya shall cloud your mind anymore. All this was Maya, all these problems; but if you get devotion, Maya is gone. Therefore, know Me to be the same as Brahman, the Supreme Being, who is without beginning, birthless, devoid of attributes, and yet a mine of transcendent, divine virtues. Listen, Kakabhushundi, devotees are always dear to Me. Realizing this, cherish unflinching devotion to My feet in thought, word, and deed.'"

"'Now, listen to My most sacred teaching, which is not only true and easily intelligible, but has also been echoed by the Vedas. I give you to hear My own conclusion; listen to it and imprint it on your mind. This is very important.

"'This world, with all its varieties of life, moving and unmoving, is a creation of My Maya. I love them all, because all are My creatures, but human beings are the dearest to Me of all. Of human beings, those that follow the course of conduct prescribed in the scriptures are My favourites. Of these latter, those who are averse to the pleasures of sense are dearer to Me, and yet more are the wise. And of the wise too, I love a man of realization all the more. And more beloved to Me even than these is My own devotee, who solely depends on Me, and has no other hope. Again and again, I repeat to you the truth that no one is so dear to Me as My devotee. The humblest creature that breathes, if possessed with devotion, is as dear to Me as life. Such is My nature.'"

"Without faith, there can be no devotion, and Sri Rama never melts except through devotion, and without Rama's grace, the human soul can never attain peace, even in a dream. Pondering thus, O Garuda, abandon all cavilling and scepticism and doubt. And adore the all-beautiful Sri Rama, a fountain of mercy and the delight of all. He is an ocean of countless virtues. Can anyone sound His depth? I have told you the little I heard from the sages. The Lord is won only by sincere devotion, and is a fountain of joy and abode of compassion. Therefore, giving up worldly attachment, vanity, and pride, one should adore that Gracious Being."

Amma On Advaita

The Hunter Who Forgot He Was a King

Once there was a king who had a battle with another king. The first king lost the battle and so he fled from the battlefield. Sometimes in the old days, if the king lost the battle, he would prefer to die on the battlefield and then ascend to the higher planes. There was nothing wrong with leaving the battlefield and then hiding out, so to say, or going underground, gaining strength and then again coming to fight with the enemy. So, this king ran away from the battlefield, and his prime minister also went with him. Since the victor was going to take over the country, the king took his wife, who was pregnant, and they rode away to escape.

As they reached an elevated place, they saw that the other king was after them. So, the minister went off in one direction, and the king decided to leave his wife somewhere. Why should she also die—and the possible heir to the throne die as well? While riding through the forest, he found a hut where some hunters were living, and so he left his wife there and kept going. Eventually, the enemy king caught up with him, and that was the end of him.

After some time, the queen gave birth to the heir, a boy, and the mother of the hunter looked after her, just like her own mother would have. Sometimes, very poor people, simple people, are the ones with noble qualities. What is called civilization is not always civilized. Sometimes the people who live in the forests are much more cultured than the people who live in the cities. So, this lady looked after the queen, but the queen never told her who she was, and after the child was born, the queen died.

The boy was raised as a hunter. When he was about twelve years old, the minister, who had escaped and was hiding, thought he would look for the heir of the king. He suspected that the boy, if there was a boy, must be somewhere. Also, the subjects were very unhappy under the rule of the intruder. While the minister was searching around with a secret party, they found the prince. They weren't sure that it was the prince, but when they followed the path that the king had taken, they came across this hut, and then found the boy who was exactly twelve years old. He looked just like the king, and had the same majestic bearing. The minister talked with the grandmother there and she said, "I don't know who the boy is, but this is what happened: a pregnant lady came here who seemed to be like royalty. Her husband had left her here, and this is her child."

The minister told the boy, "You're not a hunter, you're a prince, and this kingdom belongs to you. Now it is in the hands of the enemy, and everybody wants you to come back."

The prince said, "I'm not a prince, I'm a hunter, and I enjoy being a hunter." Then the prime minister tried to appeal to his inborn kingliness, his valour, and his sympathy towards the subjects.

In the olden days, especially in India, the system of governing was a monarchy and was hereditary. In that way, there was a certain family pride that would contribute to the king's attitude so that he would sincerely look after the subjects like his own children, and because of that, the subjects also looked upon him as their father. It wasn't like an election where somebody gets elected and then they are in power for some years, and then they step down and somebody else comes in. That is a short-lived kind of thing. Also, the people that are in power won't have the same sincerity as a person whose hereditary duty and love it is. That system has mostly disappeared. Not that it was an ideal system, but it had many advantages.

The prince was eventually awakened to his duty. He decided to go to fight. The prime minister taught him the art of warfare and got the subjects together. They fought, and won back the kingdom and everyone lived happily ever after.

So, what is the meaning of the story? It has a spiritual meaning, of course. We are the hunter boy, because we don't realize, or we have forgotten, who we really are. We came from somewhere, but we don't know where. But we're not just hunters. A hunter is one whose senses are always turned outwards, and who hunts sense objects to enjoy them. In truth, we're all kings, but of which kingdom? The kingdom of the Self, the *Atma Rajyam*. All we need is to be awakened to that fact. However, that is not enough. Although the boy in the story had been awakened to the fact that he was a prince, he also had to develop the strength and skills to fight.

Similarly, this is also our condition. We hear that we're the Atman, not the body that perishes; we are the Immortal Existence, the soul. However, that is not enough. We also have to develop the skill to fight the enemies that possess the kingdom. What are the enemies? The six inner enemies, the six foes. Our enemies are not outside; they are inside our mind: desire, anger, greed, infatuation, pride, and jealousy. These are the six main enemies that steal the kingdom of the Self away from us, and keep us as poor hunters in the forest of the sense objects.

Omkara Divya Porule

Some people think that Amma doesn't talk about Self-realization, the path of Knowledge, the teachings that tell us that we are *Brahman*, but really she does. That aspect of her teaching is in some songs of hers that are called: '*Omkara Divya Porule.*' These are Amma's words and ideas, but written down by a disciple named Swami Turiyamritananda. Everybody used to call him Puja Unni. Before any of us came to Amma, he was the first person to stay near her. At that time, he was already a renunciate. He was a teenager, but he didn't want to lead a worldly life, so he was wandering around in search of the Truth. He happened to come across Amma's village and heard that there was something divine going on there. He sought out Amma, who showered him with so much affection that he was overwhelmed and has never left since.

At that time, there was nobody there to do the daily *puja* in the little family shrine that is on the property which is now Amma's ashram. He learned how to do the puja and chant the thousand names of the Divine Mother, the *Lalita Sahasranama*, everyday. He would religiously do the puja; he wouldn't miss a day, and this went on for many years. After some years, he started writing spiritual songs—very beautiful, deep, profound poetry. Many of the Malayalam songs that we hear at the ashram were written by him. His spiritual inclination is more towards Advaita Vedanta. Many of his songs are based on that vision or attitude. Amma says that even though he had little education, by worshipping Devi every day and doing the Thousand Names without missing a day, poetic talent dawned in him.

This is called *nishta*. Nishta means to be established in a spiritual practice. One could be a *japa* nishta, which means that one always does japa. Or one could be a *dhyana* nishta, a person who is always meditating. One could be a *bhajan* nishta, a person who sings devotional songs all the time. Ultimately, we should become an *Atmanistha*, one whose mind is firmly dwelling in the Self. Steadiness is gained through repetition and regular practice. One does not need a highly developed intellect to attain a high level of spirituality. What is needed is persistent repetition and practice.

So, Unni wrote down Amma's words, and, applying his poetic talent, composed this series of songs called '*Omkara Divya Porule*.'

Why Does the Sanatana Dharma Continue to Exist?

The Vedanta philosophy is the essence of the ancient Vedic way of life or *Sanatana Dharma,* which has existed from time immemorial. Every other ancient system of philosophy either has its source in that or has disappeared. There have always been people who experienced the ultimate fruit of that way of life in the form of Self-realization. These people are called sages or mahatmas. There has always been at least one such person, at any time in history, who was a witness to the truth of the Sanatana Dharma, the path of Self-knowledge. Otherwise, like other systems, it would have died out with the coming of other systems.

There is no way to verify the truth that we are one with the indivisible, eternal, immortal, expansive, Pure Awareness or God, because we are not experiencing That as It is. Belief in that is based on the words of Self-realized sages and the Vedic scriptures. Vedanta is the teaching that occurs in the final portions of the Vedas called the Upanishads, the doctrine of Advaita or Non-duality. Vedanta declares that the ultimate goal of life is to intuitively experience that we are the Infinite and Eternal Bliss. The happiness that we are always seeking through our senses and mind can only be known when our consciousness reaches the source of both, our True Self.

In recent times, Sri Ramana Maharshi was considered by many to be a person established in Self-realization. The most recent one, whom many of us know, is Amma. She is established in the state of Brahmic Consciousness or what is traditionally known as *sahaja samadhi*, the Natural State of the Self.

Samadhi doesn't mean, as is commonly understood, to be in a trance, or that a person becomes unconscious of everything. That may be a kind of a samadhi, but Amma says that the permanent state of sahaja samadhi is what we should strive for. It is just the state of being the Atman, the all-pervading Self. In that state, whether our senses are working or not does not make any difference in our experience of Oneness.

Omkara Divya Porule is her teachings on Advaita. The first verse is,

"Come quickly, darling children,
You, who are the essence of OM."

Even though Amma is Brahman, as far as she is concerned, we are all children. At the same time, we're not only that. We are the essence of the sound OM. What is OM? OM is Brahman manifested in the plane of sound or vibration. The closest that we can get to that Unmanifest Reality in manifestation is the sound OM. That is why chanting it is so effective for stilling the mind; it takes the mind towards that state. Amma is telling us we are That—Brahman.

It is said that there are different kinds of sadhaks, different kinds of spiritual aspirants, and not everybody can immediately realize that they are Brahman merely by hearing, "Thou art That." Even if Amma were to tell most of us a thousand times, "Hey, you are Brahman," we will not feel we are That, because we haven't done the required sadhana and attained the required mental purity. One has to fulfil all the conditions, and then realization will take place when the Guru says, "Thou art That."

Some sadhaks are like gunpowder, some like charcoal, and some like wet wood. When the Guru says, "Thou art That" to those who are like gunpowder, poof—they immediately realize that they are Brahman. For those who are like charcoal, it takes a while; one has to blow on them continuously, but they will eventually burst into flames. Wet wood is also not hopeless, but a lot of exertion is needed, and even if we get the fire going, a lot of smoke comes out. However, it is possible. Why? Because everyone is potentially That.

"Removing all sorrows, grow as endearing ones and become one with the sacred syllable OM."

All beings experience some sorrow or other, some more, some less. If we didn't have any sorrow, we'd be happy. The thing that makes us seek happiness is the feeling of sorrow. Amma is saying, "How to remove sorrow? By becoming one with OM."

Amma doesn't really mean becoming one with OM as if we're not one with OM now. The hunter and the prince are not two different people. The hunter didn't become a prince, the hunter is already a prince. Similarly, we're already OM, we're already Atman or Brahman, but the experience of being That is what is needed.

Then we become endearing. A person who realizes God, even if they don't say a word, will give peace to anyone who comes near their presence. They are endearing because the dearest thing to anybody is peace. One may have everything in the world, but if the mind is not peaceful, what is the use? Real happiness is peace of mind. So, one who can give peace of mind is endearing. This is the first verse.

The next verse is,

"You are the 'I' which is in me, and I am the 'you' which is in you. The feeling of difference is due to the blindness of ignorance. In truth, nothing is separate."

This is very cryptic, and if anyone thinks that Amma is not an Advaitin, all they have to do is read this verse, because this is pure Advaita. This is very tough language, but we can't just ignore it and say, "Let's get to the easy stuff," because Amma has said this, and we should try to understand what she is talking about.

The Story of Ribhu Maharshi and Nigada

There is a story that may help us understand this verse. There was a sage long ago called Ribhu Maharshi of the Advaitic school of thought, who had a disciple named Nigada. He taught him that the feeling of 'I' that is in you, in me, and in everybody, is the same. Only the adjuncts that are surrounding the 'I' are different, i.e., the mind and body. Everyone's body is different from everyone else's, although, ultimately, they get reduced to the same thing after death. The personalities also differ. Nevertheless, the feeling of 'I' is the same in everybody, and that is the Self. However, usually our mind or attention are not fixed on 'I', but on the 'not-'I', the world.

Nigada was not spiritually ripe, but rather like charcoal; he needed some fanning. He couldn't grasp that truth. It just didn't make much sense to him. He decided, 'I prefer the path of puja and japa.' So, with the Guru's blessings, he left and settled down in a holy place, engaging himself in rituals, bhajans and other devotional practices. In fact, most of us are in that same stage of spiritual evolution. Nevertheless, our Guru will not leave us there forever, but will take us to the highest state of Self-realization however long that may take. Real devotees will not want to be ordinary people for the rest of their life; they will want to attain everlasting bliss and knowledge, and that can be attained only when they become one with the Guru through Realization.

Ribhu always kept his mind's eye on Nigada. The Guru understands when the disciples are ripe. He doesn't need to be near them to understand that.

Many times, I've been wonderstruck when I hear how Amma talks about some of her devotees or disciples who are far away. She'll say what is going on in their minds and how they're feeling. It makes one wonder what Amma really is. She certainly could not be that person who is sitting in front of us. She must be the Witness that is within each one's mind to be able to know how a person is feeling so many thousands of miles away.

Ribhu thought, 'Okay, now Nigada has had enough of sadhana and is ready for the Advaitic state.' So, Ribhu went to the village disguised as a villager. On that day, the king was going in procession on an elephant through the village where Nigada was living. Ribhu stood next to Nigada and asked, "What is going on here?"

Nigada looked at him, but didn't recognize him and said, "Can't you see? The king is coming."

"Oh, yes. Which one is the king?"

Nigada said, "What? He is coming on the elephant."

"Oh, yes. Which one is the elephant?"

Nigada exclaimed, "Are you a fool? The elephant is below, the king is above."

Ribhu looked on for some time and then said, "Ah yes, I understand, the elephant is below, the king is above. But what do you mean by above and below?"

Nigada had enough. His patience had reached its limit. He shouted, "What kind of person are you? Get down on the ground and I'll show you." The Guru got down on the ground.

Nigada climbed onto his back and said, "Now do you understand? I'm the king and I'm above, and you're the elephant and you're below."

The Guru said, "Ah, yes, now it is clear. I'm the elephant and you're the king. One more question, please."

"Yes? What do you want to know?"

"What do you mean by 'I' and 'you'?"

When he was confronted with the problem of what is the difference between 'I' and 'you' (since for me, 'I' am 'I', and for you, your 'I' is also 'I'), he realized that everybody has got the same 'I'. How was he going to say what the difference was between them? Who is 'I' and who is 'you?'

At that moment, he realized Brahman, the one 'I' everywhere and in everybody. This is the meaning of what Amma is saying, that you are the 'I' which is in me; I'm the 'you' that is in you.

> "The feeling of difference is due to the blindness of ignorance. In truth, nothing is separate."

Then why do we feel that everybody is different, that you're different, I'm different, everyone is different? Amma says it is due to the blindness of ignorance. There is a force called ignorance, *ajñana* in Sanskrit, which is preventing us from realizing that all is the One. It is also called Maya. When you think of it relative to yourself, it is called ajñana. When you think of it as the Universal Illusion, it is called Maya. That is what makes us feel everybody is different, and we don't see the Reality underlying all the differences.

Seeing Oneness in All the Cookies

A mother and father, along with their four kids, went to the circus one day. When they were about to go into the circus tent, they saw a bakery nearby. What kind of cookies do you get at a circus?

Animal cookies, of course! Seeing them, the kids said, "Daddy, daddy, we want some cookies!" So, daddy bought a whole bag of animal cookies and gave them to the children. As they were about to go into the tent, an uproar ensued. One boy took out a tiger cookie. The other one had a deer cookie.

The first boy was saying, "I'm going to eat your cookie to death." The other boy had a hawk cookie; another had a dove cookie. One was saying, "My cookie is going to tear your cookie to pieces." The strong cookie children were getting rowdy towards the weak cookie children, and there was a lot of sorrow and fighting and things were getting crazy.

The father wasn't about to give up, since they hadn't even gotten into the tent to see the real animals. He said, "Hold on, everybody get in a line." So, they all got in a line. He said, "Show me your cookies." Everybody showed their cookies. "Okay, now eat your cookies." They ate their cookies, and then realized that everybody's cookies tasted the same. The differences were just in their shapes, but the taste was the same. Then everybody was happy. No more fighting. There was peace, *shanti*. Why? Because they were paying so much attention to the form that they didn't know that the sweetness was the common essence. Similarly, this is what Amma is saying. Because we pay attention to superficial things, we miss the essence, which is the same in everybody.

The Self is Bliss

> "Find satisfaction by bathing in the Lake of the Self. To enjoy Immortal Bliss, first try to attain the Self."

Amma is pointing out that real satisfaction, real happiness, is in the Atma, not in anything else. As all of us know, from the time we're born till the time we leave the body, we're engaged in one thing only, and that is the search for happiness. When we're children, the first thing that we find happiness in is our mother; then come the toys, games, and other family members. After that, we get interested in our friends, school, career, marriage and raising a family. Then we get old and find happiness in the grandchildren and in the memories of the past, and finally, we leave the body and continue our journey, wandering around the universe always looking for happiness. It is something that we have no control over. The search for happiness is constantly making us do various things in this world.

Usually, children are happy. Why? Because their minds are unknowingly experiencing the Self more than the world. Their intellect is not developed much, so they don't recognize that experience, but they are naturally blissful and happy before their habits and desires become formed and before the world is felt to be a reality. They also have no desire to experience anything other than to be busy with what they're doing.

Sleep Holds a Clue to the Bliss of the Self

It seems like the only time that we experience happiness is when our mind becomes still after a desire is satisfied, or, when we are asleep. Sleep holds a very important clue to what Amma is talking about. She says real happiness is only in the Self. So, where is the

Self? The Self isn't somewhere out there; it is your Self or Essence. When the mind stops going outwards to things that are 'not-Self,' it rests in itself, and then happiness is experienced. This is what happens to us in sleep. Our attention or our consciousness becomes diverted completely from what is external to our Self and merges in our Self, and then we're happy.

What happens when we wake up in the morning but don't need to get up urgently? We might go back to sleep. Why? Because we were happy in sleep. Sleep is such a blissful condition; nothing can be compared to it. One could be very happy in this world, yet still, at some point, one will feel, 'Oh, forget it,' and go to sleep, because the bliss of sleep is higher than any other happiness that the senses or world can give.

The sleep state shows us that real happiness is in our self; it is not something outside us. The sleep state is, in a way, related to death. Most of us are very afraid of death. Even the slightest feeling that there is something wrong with our health makes us upset. Why? Because we subconsciously feel three things. One is that we're not going to exist anymore after death. Another is that we fear that the body is going to leave us; we're not going to have a body anymore. And, finally, that we are leaving our familiar world. But, really speaking, when we go to sleep, what are we doing? The reason we go to sleep is to forget about our body, our endless thoughts, and the world, not to be bothered with them anymore, at least for some time. The reason why sleep is so blissful is because the body and world are not there, not in our consciousness. Deep, dreamless sleep is very close to samadhi. The only difference is, samadhi is full of light—the light of awareness, and sleep is full of the darkness of ignorance—spiritual ignorance.

In this wandering about looking for satisfaction, we get exhausted. Just note how we feel when we come home after spending the whole day out there in the world? What is the best word? The word that I hear people use all the time, and the word that I also use when I have to go out there, is 'burned out'. "I feel so burned out!" And then, when we come home, or when we come to the ashram, what do we feel? Refreshed and relaxed; it is such a relief.

This search, this endless search for happiness outside, and the distractions that it entails, burn us and heats up our mind. We feel like taking a bath in cool water. That is what Amma calls the Lake of the Self, the *Atma Sarovara*. Nobody wants to be unhappy. If anybody wants to be unhappy, it is ultimately because being unhappy makes them happy! So we can't get away from wanting to be happy. And everybody wants to be happy always. Nobody wants to be miserable even for a moment. Everybody wants to be only happy *all* the time. That is the desire for eternal bliss. Amma says that if we want eternal bliss, which everyone wants, whatever name they're calling it, first try to attain it through merging in the Self.

Simplify Your Life

Most have heard the expression: "Simple living, high thinking." If our daily life and our possessions are simplified, then it is possible for our mind to get more absorbed into the Self. One thing that we could do is not be so involved in the 'not-self'. Now, that may sound like a high philosophy, but there are some practical things that we can do. Each one of us should go through our closets, our dressers, our junk drawers and everywhere that we're storing things—our basements, our attics, etc. See how much of that stuff is really necessary for us to live, and how much is just laying around to no purpose. Many of us would probably find truckloads of stuff. Sometimes I feel wonderstruck when I happen to look in a closet where we may be staying, and see the pairs of shoes, the shirts, the pants, the dresses, the saris. It is unbelievable! What we need is a couple of changes of clothes or shoes or dresses or whatever. And many people have got forty, fifty, sixty of each! And, as we also know, very many people have only one. The point is, those of us who have too much should try to simplify our lives if we want to make spiritual progress. We should decrease our possessions and share with others.

The Story of the Sadhu Who Slept On Three Stones

Does everybody know what a sadhu is? A sadhu is a saintly person or a renunciate. There was a sadhu who lived in the forest and really had minimal possessions. He had only five things: a waist cloth or dhoti, a sheet that he used to cover himself with at night, and three stones. Now what did he do with those stones? In the daytime, he put the stones on the ground in a tripod position, and would sit on them and do his meditation and studying. At night, he would put one stone under his feet, another stone under his hips, and the third stone under his head. Then he would cover himself with the sheet and go to sleep. Even if it rained, there was no problem because the water would go under him. The snakes and the scorpions also would just go through the passages. So he was very comfortable. He was having good sleep at night, and, in the daytime, he was comfortably meditating.

One day, as he was resting out in the forest, the king rode by on a hunting expedition and saw this poor sadhu laying on stones for a bed. He felt very sorry for him. When he went back to the palace, he sent some of his messengers and asked them to invite the sadhu to the palace. Usually, if a king invites us to the palace, we don't say 'no.' So the sadhu was in a fix. He didn't really want to go, but, saying, "okay," took his three stones, tied them up in the sheet and went to the palace.

When the king saw the sadhu come in, he bowed down to him and fed him sumptuously, and then took him to the royal bedroom. There was a beautiful bed about four feet thick, which had a canopy over it and silk sheets and big fluffy pillows. The king said, "Swamiji, I hope you'll be comfortable here. We'll see you in the morning. Have a good rest."

The next morning, the king came into the room, bowed down to the swami and said, "Swamiji, I hope you were comfortable."

The swami said, "How could I not be comfortable? There is nothing lacking here. Wherever I am, I'm comfortable."

The king said, "No, no, Swamiji, I don't mean that. I mean that when you were out in the forest, you were suffering so much. You were sleeping on those three stones. I couldn't bear seeing it. Now you must be very happy here enjoying all the comforts and the soft bed and everything."

The swami said, "Why, whatever I have there I have here." He pointed at the bed, and there on the bed were the three stones!

Well, we don't have to simplify that much. Don't worry. Amma doesn't expect anybody to get rid of their beds and use stones! The idea is that we could simplify our lives very much, down to the minimum. We should take that seriously. Look at Amma's life, or the life of the people who live in the ashram in India. It is very minimal, and that is all we really need anywhere in the world. We don't need too much. This is called *aparigraha* in the scriptures on yoga. That means non-possession. Non-possession means not to have more than we need. It doesn't mean that we have to walk around with nothing. We can have what we need, but not more than that.

This is one way to find satisfaction in the Self, and many of us might have experienced how having too many things distracts the mind. Sometimes even one thing is able to distract the mind. In fact, many of our lives are like that. There is a well-known story of the brahmachari and the *kaupinam* that is worth recounting because it is related to this topic.

The Brahmachari and the Kaupinam

Everybody knows what a brahmachari (celibate student) is, but I'm sure some people don't know what a *kaupinam* is. It is a loincloth that covers the private parts, somewhat like minimalist underwear. There are many pictures of sadhus in India who wear only a loincloth.

Once there was a guru and a brahmachari who were living on the outskirts of a village, and all they had was a thatched hut. The brahmachari had only two kaupinams, so, after he took his bath in the morning, he would change the wet one and wear the dry one. Then he would wash it and put it up on top of the roof to dry. One day, the guru said, "I feel like going on a pilgrimage. I'll come back after sometime. You stay here and do your sadhana."

So the guru went, and the brahmachari was doing his sadhana, but some rats started eating his kaupinams. He didn't know what to do. When he went to the village to beg his food, he told the villagers, "My kaupinams are getting eaten by rats and have holes. What should I do?"

They said, "Why don't you get a cat? Cats eat rats."

He said, "That is a good idea, but where from is a brahmachari to get a cat?" Somebody donated a cat. Everything was all right for a little while, but there weren't that many rats, so the cat was getting hungry. When he went to town the next time, he told some of his sponsors, "I've got this cat; it is always making a racket at the ashram because there are not enough rats to eat, and there is nothing else for me to give it."

Then somebody said, "Why don't you get a cow? Then you can give that milk to the cat." So somebody donated a cow. Now he had the cow, but to look after a cow is a lot of work. One has to do so many things.

A brahmachari doesn't have the time for all those things. He is meditating, reading the scriptures and doing his japa. Somebody suggested that he get a servant to look after the cow, and so he got a servant. However, the servant had a big family, and so they had to construct some living quarters for the servant. The servant brought his relatives, and, eventually, one single hut became a sprawling mansion with dozens of people there. Does this sound familiar? Many of us have undertaken something for a simple reason that becomes very complicated. What started out as a very simple life for the brahmachari, turned out to be his living in a big mansion surrounded by animals and servants!

After many years, the guru came back from his pilgrimage. He didn't see the hut anywhere, so he asked the villagers, "Has anybody seen my disciple?"

They said, "Oh yes, he is out there on the outskirts of the village. See that sprawling mansion with all the servants running around? That is where your brahmachari lives."

The guru went there and shouted his brahmachari's name. The brahmachari came out dressed in a silk robe and bowed down to the guru. The guru said, "What happened to you?"

The disciple thought about it and replied, "It was all because of that kaupinam!"

People get into relationships or undertakings, and then, years later, wonder how their life became so complicated. The ocean of birth, death and rebirth is vast. It is not easy to keep things simple, but we should try if we want peace of mind.

Amma never says not to enjoy life. She doesn't tell everybody to become celibate brahmacharis or sannyasis. She says to enjoy life, but at the same time, to remember this: Maya will always cause complications. So enjoy, but temper it with the knowledge that there are going to be inevitable complications and suffering mixed in with the pleasures. We should not jump into worldly life thinking that is the solution to the problem of attaining happiness, thinking everything is going to be all right. How many times do we hear people say, "I'm still searching for the right person, the right job, the right house, and I know that they should exist, but problems always arise." Isn't that the case? There is no such thing as the right person, the right job, the right lifestyle or the right anything, because everything is intrinsically limited and has defects. Lasting happiness is a dream that can never come true from changing things. Even then, we should have a good time as far as possible, and ultimately come back to the Self, which is where real happiness is.

The Purpose of Human Birth is Absorption In the Self

> "Merge in yourself to become one with Me, and always seek happiness there. In order to remove all sorrows and to fulfil this birth, get absorbed in the Pure Self. Amma is the servant of servants and has no abode of her own. Her real dwelling place is in your inmost Self."

Real happiness is in the Self. When we become disillusioned with all the other so-called happinesses outside the Self, only then will we seek happiness where it really is, in our real Self. Amma says that if you merge in your Self, then you become one with her. Why? Because the real Amma is not only the Amma that is living in Amritapuri, or the Amma who travels around the world. The real Amma is the innermost Self of each one of us. If we merge in our Self, then we will find her. That is where the end of all sorrows is. That is the Immortal Bliss.

To do this means to fulfil the purpose of our birth. Having attained a human birth, a human body, as opposed to a non-human plant body, animal body or even a celestial body, is the last stage of evolution. After that, the only purpose in life is to realize that the bliss that we're seeking is in our Self, not anywhere else. Many find happiness in Amma's presence because she is constantly radiating the Self. In her presence, our mind becomes calm and we effortlessly experience a glimpse of the happiness that is the Self.

Sorrow Leads Us to God

Amma says to remove all sorrows, we should get absorbed in the pure Self. Some people ask why God gives us sorrow. If there is a God, He must be a cruel being, because living beings are suffering in this world. Amma says that sorrow has a purpose. One purpose is for us to pay the price for the negative actions that we do; this is the law of Nature. Mother Nature is like a mirror. Whatever we do gets reflected back at us. If we do things disharmonious with Nature, our body or mind suffer. This is one reason for sorrow. The other reason is to wake us up from the sleep of Maya so that we can realize the Self, or at least start on the path back to our Source.

Remembrance of God in Times of Sorrow

"Queen Kunti prayed to the Lord that she should be sorrowful all the time. She did so, because she felt she would remember the Lord more in sorrow than in prosperity. Amma feels that, in the light of the sun, you see

The Self is Bliss

all objects, but you never notice the sun. Contrarily, in the moonlight you see only the moon. It is the same in the darkness of sorrow, you see the Lord. In the light of the sun you see only material objects, but in the moonlight, the same objects are there, but one only sees the moon. Similarly, in the darkness of sorrow, you think only of the Supreme."

Story of Bhartruhari

Nothing about Bhartruhari is definitely known to history except that he was of Indian royalty in the 5th century A.D., the elder brother of the famous King Vikramaditya of Ujjain in central India and was a renowned poet. He was both very worldly and very spiritual at the same time. The story goes that a yogi gave him a divine mango that he had manifested through his own spiritual power and told the king, "If you eat this, you'll live for a very long time. As you are royalty, I think that you are the fittest person to have this mango. If a righteous king lives for a long time, then the subjects also will be happy."

Bhartruhari took the mango. He thought, 'The dearest thing to me is my queen. What is the use of my living hundreds of years if my queen is going to die? It is better my queen lives a long life and retains her beauty so that I can enjoy her until I die.' So he called his queen and gave her the mango, saying, "If you eat this, you will live hundreds of years."

What did the queen do with the mango? She had a boyfriend. We shouldn't be surprised. Everywhere and always in this world, people have boyfriends and girlfriends. The queen's boyfriend worked in the stables. She called him and said, "It is better if you live a long life so that I can enjoy you. Eat this divine mango," and she gave the mango to him.

The stable boy also had another girlfriend, and so he gave the mango to her. She also had another boyfriend, and so she gave it to him, and this went on and on. Finally, the mango made its way into the hands of a prostitute. She thought that Bhartruhari would be a more deserving person than herself, and so she went to the royal court and gave it to him.

The king asked, "What is this?"

She replied, "This is a divine mango. If you eat this, you will live hundreds of years."

Needless to say, Bhartruhari was a little surprised. He made some enquiries, and it came back that his queen wasn't so faithful as he thought. This came as a tremendous shock to him, which woke him up from the sleep of Maya, realizing, as he now did, the true nature of human love.

Leaving the kingdom, he went to a cave and spent the rest of his life there doing sadhana and, from what his poetry reveals, probably attained Self-realization. Being an accomplished poet, he wrote a poem of one hundred verses describing his observations about worldly existence and his hard-fought struggles and victories over his sensual nature. The poem is called *Vairagya Satakam* or *A Hundred Verses on Detachment*.

His sorrow obviously bore fruit by liberating him from all illusions, and that is the ultimate purpose of suffering, i.e., to teach us that the long dream of worldly existence will end only when we finally turn away from it towards the Self.

Fours Aims of Human Life

In ancient India, the sages promulgated the philosophy of *Purushartha*, which was practiced by everyone and enforced by the king. Purusharthas are the four proper goals or aims of human life. They are *Dharma* (righteousness, moral values), *Artha* (prosperity, economic values), *Kama* (pleasure, love, enjoyment) and *Moksha* (liberation, release from the cycle of rebirths). The nature and implication of the ultimate goal of life, Self-realization or Moksha, was taught from childhood. However, being ordinary human beings with desires and ambitions, most people should go through the first three stages before becoming fit for full renunciation and dedication to spiritual realization. First comes education, training, serving and discipline, which are called *brahmacharyashrama*. Then comes marriage, enjoying the pleasures of life, business, children and family known as *grihastashrama*. After that, doing *tapas* and *sadhana*, called *vanaprastha* or forest dwelling, and only then comes complete renunciation or *sannyasa*. This system put the soul on the path of gradual evolution towards Self-reailzation.

Children Should Experience the World

When we're talking about the unreality of the world, the philosophy of *jñana*, none of us, especially the youngsters, should get confused and think that we're saying that we shouldn't enjoy the world. That is not what we're saying at all. We should enjoy the world. However, we should also understand that the final goal of life is possible only when we experience union with God. If we don't enjoy the world, we won't know what the world is all about. Then how or why will we turn towards the Self or God? We are not trying to discourage anyone from enjoying life; we're just trying to make everybody aware that the real goal is God.

> "Like the blue of the sky and the water of the distant mirage in the desert, remember that this world is unreal brought forth by the magic of Illusion."

When we look up at the sky, it looks blue, but really it is not. Have you ever driven through a desert? Did you see a mirage? When we're driving on a hot day, we may see water or even other objects at a distance even though they aren't there. That is called a mirage, an unreal image. If we get out of the car and run to the water, what will we find? Nothing!

Amma is saying to remember that this world is just like that. It appears to be full of what we want, but it is not. It is not real. If it was real, then we should be able to get the satisfaction that we want, but nobody has an experience of lasting satisfaction through anything. That is why it is called Maya. It seems to be real, but it isn't.

Therapists Can Help Up to a Point

(Swami): Does anyone feel the philosophy that we're talking about is too tough?

(Audience response): I'd like to say something.

(Swami): Yes?

(Audience response): I relate to what you're talking about. I've been chasing these illusions my whole life, thinking that is where happiness is, but, until now, I never quite caught it. In relationships and business and money, you name it! I had a lot of material things and relationships. Happiness was there for a while, and then it disappeared. It never lasted. None of it! But the pull of Maya is very, very powerful. You think it is there. It looks like it is there. Yet it almost disappears right before your eyes. And then comes sorrow and blaming yourself and wondering. You end up with a therapist. And the therapist also is trying to figure out what happened.

(Swami): That is exactly what Amma says. The only therapist who could fix us is one who herself doesn't need therapy. Therapy has its uses, but for solving this big problem of being happy, only one who is completely happy can show us the way. The only one who fits that description is a Realized soul, a true Master.

Nobody else can show us the way, and it can't be shown or known through books. We can read any number of books written about self-improvement, Self-realization or spirituality, but it cannot be found in there, either. Those are only hints.

Lasting happiness can be found only through the company of a God-realized soul and through their grace. Their company would greatly benefit us, but we must strive to make ourselvest receptive to their grace. We could live with a mahatma, we could have their blessings, but if our mind is not open to that, if we don't follow their teachings, then we can't get out of the morass of the Universal Illusion.

We go through a lifetime of seeking happiness, and finally return to where we started, none the wiser. Then death comes and the whole fruitless journey starts again. So, where is the end to it? What is the meaning of life? These are very serious questions. We should be thinking about these even from the time we're youngsters.

What is the purpose of life? Why is nobody thinking about anything deeper than the immediate thing that is in front of them? We can live a normal life, but we should temper it with such thoughts. 'I'm a subject in the kingdom of Maya. How can I break out so that I'm in the kingdom of God?' That is the purpose of our association with Amma and trying to learn Amma's teachings.

The World Is Unreal

This world seems to be real, but there is no real happiness in it. The happiness that we seek from the world doesn't exist there; it is not in any object. It is within us, in the Atma, in the Self. When the mind becomes concentrated through pleasure, it becomes quiet, and happiness is experienced. When a desired object is attained or an unwanted object is removed, the resulting peace is happiness. It is not because of any object outside us, although objects trigger it.

Look On the World as a Dream

This way of looking at things—that this is all a long dream—is one way for us to progress spiritually towards the experience of Reality. It is also a very practical way for us to get peace of mind in the distracting world that we live in.

Once, I was visiting a family along with a sannyasi, and there was a very—I guess the word would be—"obnoxious" person there. They were constantly shouting and screaming and arguing, a very loud person creating a very agitated atmosphere. I had never experienced a place like this.

I felt very distracted and struggled with that for two or three days. I just kept saying to myself, 'Well, it is God in that form. Why should I get upset?' But somehow, that didn't help very much. Then I asked the sannyasi, who seemed to be perfectly calm, "How are you able to stay calm in this uproar?"

He said, "Why do you give so much reality to that person? It is just a dream." I thought about that. I realized that it was true. The more that I reacted to it, the more that I gave importance to it, the more it was disturbing me. Then I decided, 'Yes, this is just a dream,' and became peaceful again even in the midst of that thunderstorm!

If we can live in the present as if what is happening now happened thirty years ago, with that much detachment, then there will be no identification with anything at all. Whatever might happen really doesn't cause any feelings in us, because we are separated by so much time and space. Similarly, if we can live today with the sense that this is all a dream, that this will all pass away, then the agitations that we suffer from will be much less.

Amma says to remember this world is unreal, brought forth by the magic of Maya. What does she mean by 'unreal'? Or, what is meant by the word 'real'? In the Upanishads, the word 'real' or 'sat', is defined as:

> "Reality is that which is always the same. It eternally exists as It is and never changes."

In our experience, there is nothing that doesn't change. There is nothing that is always the same—except one thing. And that one thing is the most important thing for this discussion. It is also the one thing that we overlook all the time, because it is the most obvious.

To understand what that one thing is in us which doesn't change, we shouldn't look outside. There is nothing outside us that doesn't change. Mother Nature always changes. In fact, *prakriti*, which is what the word in Sanskrit is for Nature, means:

> "That which changes, that which is always transforming."

There is nothing outside us that we can look for that doesn't change. So, where to look for 'sat'; where to look for reality? Inside us! What is there inside us that doesn't change? We must try to analyse our daily experience.

The Three States

The Upanishads say we have three states that we pass through every day. What are they? Waking, dreaming and dreamless sleep. We are aware of our waking state; in the dream, we are aware of the dreams; in deep sleep, we are aware of the nothingness of deep sleep, even though we are unable to remember it clearly. There is some kind of awareness, some kind of experience even in dreamless sleep. Otherwise, nobody would be able to say that they had a sound sleep. All they could say is, "Well, I dreamt, and after that, I don't know what happened." So we do know what happened in sound sleep—there is some subtle experience of peace and rest and bliss. 'That', which is witnessing these three constantly changing states is the Reality.

Reality is not some far-away thing; it is not some being apart from us; it is the awareness that is 'us,' which never changes. However, we always overlook that. We're always busy with the pictures, not with the Observer. We're always busy with the changing scenes; we miss the screen on which they are projected. We go to see a movie, or watch the TV. If the screen wasn't there, there would be no pictures at all. The screen is not affected by anything that is going on in the pictures. There may be a fire, there may be a flood, there may be shooting, there may be anything. Similarly, without awareness, there is no experience, and even though the experiences are there, they don't really affect awareness. Nothing can destroy it. Nothing can change it. Things can affect the mind—the mind is the instrument of cognition—but it is not the awareness itself.

This awareness is the thing that is real in us. The thing that is unreal, the thing that changes, is our experience: the waking state, the dream state, the deep sleep state. Amma is advising us to remember that this world is unreal, because, by doing so, we won't give so much importance to it. It is because of giving it so much importance, so much reality to the world, that we suffer.

All This Will Pass Away

One way to develop that sense is to think, 'Everything will pass away—all this will pass away—nothing will ever be here forever.' There is a story about this very thing.

There was a merchant who wanted his son to be educated abroad and get a good job there. When the son was about to go, he gave him a diamond ring and said, "Son, take this ring. I don't know if I'll ever see you again, because I'm already an old man. Whenever you're very troubled in your heart, go off in a corner and take off the ring and just play with it. Just throw it up and down and remember how much affection I had for you, how much I was concerned about you. This is why I am giving you this ring, out of my love for you. So, just play with it in a corner."

Then the son thought, 'What strange advice my father is giving—but I'll show respect to him. I'll wear the ring and follow his advice.'

So, he went abroad and got his education there. Soon, he got a good job and became a very successful businessman. Unfortunately, everything started going wrong. He tried his best, but he couldn't revive his business. He was running into deep debt. He was ashamed to write to his father for help. He didn't see any solution to his problems, and so he decided to kill himself.

He just wanted to be rid of his suffering, so he climbed up on a bridge and was about to jump, when he saw the ring on his finger. He remembered, 'My father told me that when I'm very agitated, I should take off the ring and play with it for some time. Anyhow, these are my last moments. Out of respect for him, let me do it.'

So he climbed off the bridge. There was a lamp post there. He sat under the light, took off the ring, and started to play with it. As he was playing with it, he noticed there was something written on the inner edge. He looked closely at the ring and it said, "All this will pass away." Then he started thinking, 'All this will pass away. That is true! All this will pass away. Even my terrible situation, even my misery and my suffering—all that will pass away.' And the more he thought about it, the more silly he felt that he had wanted to escape the situation without trying to solve it.

He got in his car, drove back home, and began thinking how he got into this whole mess, and found a way out. Gradually, his business picked up after that, and everything became all right. But even after that, he didn't forget what the ring said: "All this will pass away." Not only will the unpleasant things pass away; the pleasant things also will pass away. So he wasn't overly happy about his prosperity. He wasn't miserable about poverty either.

This is one thing that we can do to keep our mind balanced and even—to not allow the sense of reality to be so strong in the changing circumstances of our life, think that, "All this will pass away."

> "Don't spend your time uselessly, forgetting the purpose for which you have come to this world. Try to be aware of the Atma each and every moment."

Most of us spend our whole life busy with things other than the purpose for which we're born as a human being. It is told in the scriptures that only a human being can attain the goal of existence, which is Self-realization. Animals and plants can rarely attain it only through Divine grace or the grace of a Guru, but they can't make any conscious effort towards that. Their existence is completely conditioned by their animal or plant nature. Whereas, human beings can improve; they can purify their minds. They can meditate. They can practice various spiritual disciplines. And then they can attain the vision of God, or Self-realization. That will be the end of their spiritual evolution. But what Amma is saying here is that most human beings don't do that. They lead just an ordinary, mundane existence, and play just ordinary music, so to say.

Story of the Master Organ Player

Once there was an organ in a church and there was only one person who was allowed to play it. One day, an old man walked into the church. The service was over and everybody was walking out, so he asked if he could play on the organ. The people in charge of the church said, "Absolutely not. Only the organ player can play on the organ." So he hid in a corner, and when everybody was just about out, he ran up the stairs and started playing on the organ. The music was divine! Everybody came back and sat in their seats. They listened for an hour to his music. It turned out that he was the inventor of the organ, although he seemed like just a poor fellow.

Similarly, we're busy playing mundane music, and that is all that comes out of most of us. The one who really knows how to play the organ of our body isn't allowed in there to play the divine music, because we are busy all the time with ordinary, day-to-day affairs. So we should try to become an organ in the hands of the Maker. The inventor of the organ, the inventor of the body, is God. Then we'll play beautiful music.

Greatness of the Divine Name

> "Blessed will be this human birth, if the technique of meditation through chanting the Divine Name and

mantra of the Lord is learned, thereby extinguishing the disease of attraction and repulsion."

While talking about trying to attain Self-realization, it is all well and good to say that we should be established in the Self, that we should look upon the world as unreal, that we shouldn't get either overly attracted by anything or repulsed by anything else, that we should keep an even mind. But somehow, when situations arise, we forget all that.

We might have heard the story about the parrot that was kept in a cage by a priest. This parrot would always say, "Rama Rama Rama," because the *pujari* would always repeat, "Rama Rama Rama" while performing the worship. But then, one day, a cat got in and opened the cage and tried to catch the bird. The bird shrieked, "Aaaaar!" Forgetting all about Rama, his old nature returned.

Similarly, we think about devotion and jñana, but when any little thing causes us to worry, away goes our spiritual understanding. Not that it should, but that is what happens.

Amma is giving us a practical and concrete way to strengthen our mind. That is mantra japa or the Name of God. The principle is this: our mind is always busy thinking. Always. Not even for a moment does it stop thinking, except at one time, that is, when it becomes still immediately after some desire is satisfied, or, when we fall into deep sleep.

This restless mind is the very thing that makes it impossible for us to attain the vision of God, or Self-realization. And this restless mind is also the thing that makes us sad. Amma says that when the mind becomes calm, the vision of God can arise. How to make the mind calm? Instead of letting it constantly think so many diverse thoughts, give it one thought to be occupied with. Then it will slowly hold onto that one thought; it will become

The World is Unreal

strong in that one thought, and then be able to resist the many other thoughts.

Usually, when we say a person has a strong mind, we mean that they're able to think a lot. But in spiritual life, a strong mind means a mind that can resist thinking. There is a big difference. The way to achieve it is to use the nature of the mind to always think, but to think of only one thing rather than many things. Then the mind becomes more and more calm, and gradually, the reflection of God's presence or the Atma dawns in that calm mind.

Instances of Great Devotees

Devotion is very necessary for us to be able to practice japa like that. The ancient sage Narada Maharshi wrote a philosophical work called the *Narada Bhakti Sutras*. It is a very well-known work on devotion, and it is interesting how he came to write it, since he was previously a jñana yogi. He liked the path of jñana, the path of knowledge, always holding onto the feeling 'I am', trying to keep the mind established in the Self.

Narada observed that of all His devotees, Bhagavan Sri Krishna had the most affection for the gopis of Brindavan. He wondered, 'What is so great about the gopis? They're always just repeating the name of Krishna.' They used to go through the streets, and when selling milk, yogurt and ghee, instead of saying, "Milk," "Yogurt," and "Ghee," they would say, "Krishna," "Narayana," and "Madhava." They would forget what it was they were doing and were always immersed in singing the Divine Name.

When Narada went to Brindavan, the gopis recognized him. They bowed down to him, did puja to him and showed great respect to him. Then he started to talk to them about the path of knowledge.

He said, "You should all be walking in the path of knowledge. You're all ripe devotees, fit to attain the highest Self-realization even now."

They said, "Narada, we don't want to hear anything about the path of knowledge. The path of devotion is enough for us. We don't need your knowledge. Rama, Krishna, Hari, Govinda, Narayana—that is enough for us."

He was watching their daily life for some days. They were full of the Name of God. Their mind never wavered, even a little bit. Seeing that, he got so inspired that he decided to write a book called the *Bhakti Sutras*, the Nature of Bhakti, and that became one of the classics of devotional literature.

Through mantra japa, the gopis attained Self-realization. Amma says that we should repeat our mantra until there is nothing left in us, no other thoughts except the mantra. Some people ask, "I got a mantra from Amma. How much should I repeat it?" There is no question of how much. There is no upper limit. One should repeat it all the time if one can. It should be the last thing before falling asleep and the first thing when waking up. It should be on our lips when we leave the body at death.

The Great Crow Devotee

Lord Rama and Lakshmana were standing by the side of a lake and saw a crow that would dip its beak into the water, and, without drinking anything, would again pull its beak up. It kept doing this, up and down, and it couldn't drink any of the water. Then Lakshmana asked Rama, "What is this? What is wrong with this crow?"

Rama said, "This is one of My greatest devotees."

Lakshmana said, "What is so great?"

"Can't you see? He is repeating My name all the time, even though he is dying of thirst. When he goes to the water to get a drink, he thinks, 'If I drink, I'm going to have to stop repeating the Divine Name and I'll miss one mantra.' So he decides not to drink the water. In this way, he hasn't been able to drink water in many days."

That kind of dedication to mantra japa is necessary if we want to become full of our mantra. That doesn't mean that we should stop eating and drinking!

> "If the mind is devoid of renunciation, great suffering will befall one through Maya. If desire is not uprooted, affliction follows, which will culminate in the ruin of anyone in this world."

If the mind is devoid of renunciation, then we'll end up in so much trouble, living in this world of Maya. Amma doesn't say that we have to renounce everything externally. That is impractical for most of us. Some great sages of the present day, and even of the past, were all living in the world. In fact, all of us are living in the world to some degree, or else we wouldn't be here at all. Renunciation means to be inwardly detached, despite how or where we're living.

We Become What We Always Think Of

> "Dear children, always remember in your heart that God is love. By meditating upon that Embodiment of Love, you also will become love personified."

The *Mahabharata* is a story of the struggle between good and evil. One of the main characters, Duryodhana, persecutes his innocent cousins, the Pandavas, his whole life until his death. He did only bad things. Perhaps he wasn't so bad at the time of his birth. Unfortunately, he had very bad company—an uncle named Shakuni. Amma feels that Shakuni was one of the causes of all the trouble that happened in the *Mahabharata*.

All of us sometimes act like Shakuni. We may have a grudge towards somebody. Then we start to talk about them in a negative way, and that influences other's minds. If somebody constantly tells us something bad about someone, eventually we also start to believe it.

Similarly, Duryodhana was always hearing from his uncle that he should be the king, that he should take the kingdom, that he should kill his cousins, and so on, and so eventually did it.

Story of Valmiki

Then there was Valmiki. He was previously known as Ratnakaran. He was also not a good person; he was a thief. He killed many people. Once he tried to steal from some sages who were walking through the forest. I don't know what he was trying to steal from them, because usually the sages that were living in the forests had almost nothing except for the fruits and roots that they were eating. Nevertheless, through their association, he became so great that he wrote the *Ramayana*.

They asked him, "Why are you killing and stealing?"

He replied, "Because I have to support my family."

"Do you know how much sin you're getting by killing people like this?"

"Yes, I know."

"Do you think that your family is going to share all that with you?"

"I don't know, I never thought of that."

"Well, why don't you go ask your family whether they're going to share the bad karma that you're getting by supporting them in this way."

So he tied them up to trees, and said that he would go ask.

He went and asked his wife and his children. "Do you know how I've been supporting you?"

"No."

"I've been stealing and killing to get the money to support you. Are you willing to share some of the bad karma that I'm getting from doing these things?"

"No way! Absolutely not! We didn't ask you to do that."

That was a big shock for him. He went running back and fell at the feet of the sages and untied them. He said, "Oh, God, what have I done with my whole life? I never even thought about it. Now, save me from my fate!"

The sages initiated him into a mantra, a very easy mantra, "Rama." He was trying to repeat "Rama," but it wouldn't come out of his mouth, because he had so much bad karma that his tongue couldn't even repeat the name of God. So the sages said, "All right, we'll give you a different mantra, 'Mara.'"

Mara means a tree. But if we say, "Mara, Mara, Mara, Mara," long enough, it becomes, "Rama, Rama, Rama, Rama."

So, unknowingly he was repeating Rama's name. He was very intense about it. People that lead an intense life, even an intensely bad life, may make quick spiritual progress once they get an awakening. It is the intensity that is important. When, in the core of their hearts, they feel they have to purify themselves, to do something to change their life, that death is around the corner, then they become serious. Then the same intensity that they were enjoying life with, or the intensity that they were doing bad things with, will become an asset.

Valmiki had that kind of intensity. He sat there and started repeating, "Mara, Mara, Mara," and continued that for many years. The story goes that an anthill (*valmika*) grew around and over him, and, eventually, he attained Divine Knowledge. He even wrote the *Ramayana*, the story of Sita and Rama, which is still read today by millions of devotees. He was worse than an ordinary person, but developed divine power through the association with sages.

Amma is saying that if we meditate on the Embodiment of Love, what will happen? We will also become love personified, which is the nature of God. If we can think of God in some form, some loving form, and mentally associate with that as much as we can, then we'll also become transformed into that. For us, Amma is there; we don't have to look very far for an embodiment of love. Just as the sun always gives light, similarly, nothing comes out of Amma except love. Anything that she says, anything that she does, has only one motive, and that is love, for the good of mankind and all living beings.

If we think of her life, then we can become like her also. We are very fortunate, because Amma leads an exemplary life all the time. We have so many examples to think of. 'How did Amma act in this situation? What did she say in that situation? What should I do in this situation?' We have a person that we can always be comparing our lives to. We can always be polishing our rough gem, so to say, against the grinding stone of Amma's example, until we become like her.

When we meditate on Amma's love, it is hard to think of any one incident that shows Amma's nature as love more than any other one. For me, I always think of the incident of when she was a young girl, and her brother and her cousin decided to do away with her. That incident shows the tremendous selfless love she has. They locked her in a room and tried to kill her, and instead of killing her, the person who actually put the knife up to her throat collapsed. Something happened inside him, something burst inside his chest at that moment.

They took him to the hospital. And what did Amma do the next day? She went to the hospital to visit this person who tried to kill her for no reason! She cooked food for him, and with her own hands, she fed him, and rubbed his forehead, just like she rubs the foreheads of so many of us, and called him, "Son."

And what happened to him? This man was merciless and as hard as a rock, but his mind melted and he burst into tears, repenting for what he had tried to do to Amma. Because of the love shown to him, his heart was purified. Could any of us even conceive of doing what she did if somebody tried to murder us the day before? Would we go to the hospital to feed them and to comfort them the next day? No human would ever even think of such a thing, much less do it. For me, this is the incident in Amma's life that shows to what extent Amma is the embodiment of love.

Selfishness

"A sadhak should not have even a trace of selfishness. Selfishness is like worms that suck the honey from the flowers. If worms are allowed to grow there, the fruit will be infested with them. There is no use of such fruit. Likewise, if selfishness is allowed to grow, it will gnaw away at all our good qualities."

The reason that Amma stresses on our negative qualities is so that we can become aware of them and remove them. We should not mull over, or think all the time about our negative qualities, but should just study them a bit so that we can recognize them when they come up and then deal with them, the way Amma advises us to.

In the distant past, we were in union with the Universal Being; we were immersed in bliss. Propelled by the Divine Will, our consciousness, which was merged in its source and blissful, became externalized and started seeking happiness there rather than from its source.

The Inner Significance of the Ramayana

In the *Ramayana*, Sita and Rama were exiled to the forest by Rama's father at the behest of Rama's stepmother, Kaikeyi. While there, Sita was kidnapped by the demon Ravana, and then Rama brought her back after killing him. That is the whole *Ramayana* in short.

Sita was very happy with Rama in Ayodhya. "Ayodhya" means "a place where there is no *yuddha* (war, conflict). Rama represents the Paramatman—God, and Sita, the *jivatman* or individual soul,

Selfishness

who was very happy and content with Rama. Even when they were exiled to the forest, they were still very happy.

One day, Sita saw a golden deer with silver spots. It wasn't an ordinary deer. It was very strange looking, but very attractive. In fact, it was a demon sent by Ravana to lure away Rama and his brother Lakshmana so that he could kidnap her. She told them, "I've got to get that deer at any cost." She forgot about the perfect happiness she enjoyed with Rama, and now her source of happiness became the golden deer, that enchanting object that looked like it would make her happy. So Rama left to catch the deer.

Hearing an anguished cry, Sita told Lakshmana to go help Rama, but he said that it could not be Rama, since Rama was all-powerful. Unwilling to listen to him, she insulted him by imputing some bad motives to him and insisted that he go. Lakshmana's advice to Sita represents the words of wise people, the scriptures or Guru, to the deluded jiva: Don't be fooled by the golden deer, it is not what it seems. You're going to get in trouble; stick to Rama.

As soon as she sent Lakshmana away, in came Ravana, a ten-headed demon. What do the ten heads represent? He represents the ego, the personality that identifies with the body and its ten sense organs. When we run after the illusory and attractive deer of sense objects, Ravana, the ego, catches us. Then we identify with the body and mind. Following that, things get complicated and it takes many, many lifetimes to get back to where we started, that blissful Ayodhya with Rama.

So what did Sita do after being kidnapped? She felt really bad and decided, 'I'm going to hold onto the thought of Rama day and night until I reach Him, until I return to Him. However much Ravana tempts me, I'm not going to pay attention to him.' This is the attitude of an ideal sadhak who doesn't swerve from their goal once they've realized that they were played the fool by Maya, by the extroverted mind. They take a firm decision, 'I'm not going to dance to the tune of Maya anymore. I'm going to hold onto God until I reach Him, however long it takes.'

Long ago, when our attention turned outwards because of the power of Maya or *avidya* (spiritual ignorance), we forgot that we are the blissful Self, the Immortal Being. That knowledge got veiled (*avarana*) and made us feel, 'I am this limited body and personality.' At the same time, we became distracted and restlessly occupied with diversity(*vikshepa*). Yet we have not completely lost the sense of God or Reality. We start to seek the bliss of the Self outwardly. That outward movement is called *pravritti* (evolution). Returning to the source is called *nivritti* or involution. These two sum up the pilgrimage of the soul.

When we are on the path of pravritti, we are unknowingly trying to realize the Self through the enjoyment of sense objects. What happens when we enjoy sense objects, any sense object? For a moment, our mind get agitated or attracted by the sense object. We want to get it, we want to enjoy it, and when we do get it or enjoy it or experience it, the mind becomes concentrated and followed by a feeling of calmness for a while. That calmness is the source of our mind. That is a reflection of the Self. To get that moment of calmness and concentration, we go through all the activities that we do, day and night. That constant search for it outside creates a habit, and because we do get a glimpse of the Self through that, we become very possessive about it. If we get happiness through a piece of chocolate cake, and somebody looks at our chocolate cake, we become very possessive about it. We hide the chocolate cake, because we got so much pleasure from it. Suppose we have a partner, and somebody else looks at them; we feel jealous or even angry, because our happiness may

Selfishness

be taken away, the happiness that we get from that person. It may be anything—our money or our house or whatever.

Why is that happiness so coveted? Because it is rare. We become selfish. We want to hold onto all these little means that we have to experience happiness. What Amma says is that by doing so, the illusion that we are an ego and a perishable body gets stronger and stronger, harder and harder, and this involves us in all kinds of mischief. Then the law of karma, or cause and effect, comes into play, because that is the law that rules this world of illusion. Sometimes we're happy, sometimes we're sad; sometimes we go up, sometimes we go down. Sometimes we're born as a human being, sometimes not as a human being.

This is the reason why selfishness is being given so much importance by Amma. Even though few know the nature of the Universal Being, everybody has an intuitive feeling that what is universal is good and what is selfish is bad. If we see some kind of selfishness, or some kind of meanness in somebody, immediately our mind condemns them; we don't like that. Nobody likes a selfish or mean person.

If we see somebody who is sharing and good natured, immediately we feel sympathy towards them; we like them. Those qualities are reflecting the Self, and we have an intuitive feeling about it. All the great people have been those who manifested qualities of the Universal Self, and we can see the very epitome of that, the embodiment of that, in a Realized soul like Amma, whose whole life is selfless or selfless existence embodied.

The more that we try to become happy in this way— in a selfish way—the more unhappy we become. It is very strange. And finally we become so miserable that maybe God or a guru shows us the way to get out of it. But sometimes we have to get to the very bottom before we can go up.

What is the cure for this selfishness? Selflessness, of course. Giving. Instead of taking and grasping and holding, give and share. An attitude of surrender also softens the ego.

Misers don't have much intelligence except for making more and more money. There was a man who used to bury his gold in his backyard, and every day he would go there and dig with a shovel and gaze at the gold, and feel so happy. That was his happiness, to look at the gold. Then one day, some thieves saw him doing that and later stole it. When he came the next day and dug up the hole, there was no gold, so he started crying. Hearing his crying, the neighbours asked, "What's the matter?"

"All my gold was stolen."

"For all the good that it was doing you, what is the difference? Before it was in the hole and now it is in somebody else's pocket. You weren't using it, so why are you so upset?" Such is the nature of a miser.

Story of Ebeneezer Scrooge

Ebeneezer Scrooge was a very selfish character. He was a miser of misers. He had a partner whose name was Marley. Both of them were extremely miserly. A miser is a person who won't make others happy with their money, nor will they allow themselves to be happy with it. The only happiness—if it could be called that—which they have, is in being miserly.

Ebeneezer Scrooge and Marley weren't just misers; they were also really mean. Perhaps these two qualities are frequently found in the same person. They would make their employees work themselves to the bone, and give them hardly a pittance, almost nothing for their labour.

In predominantly Christian countries, Christmas is the most important holiday. It is celebrated even by people of other

Selfishness

religions. In that way, it is somewhat like Onam in Kerala or Deepavali in northern India. Everybody is in a festive and giving mood, and most employees are sent home early to celebrate. But Scrooge and Marley would make their staff work till the last moment on Christmas Eve!

One day, Marley died and Scrooge took over the business completely. He became even more miserly. It was the day before Christmas and Scrooge went to sleep. In a dream, the wall behind his bed opened and a green, slimy, weird kind of bogeyman came out—some kind of monster that looked human-like.

Scrooge screamed, "Help! Who are you? What are you?"

"I'm Marley, your partner. And do you know why I became like this? Because of the miserly way that I lived! That miserly life has caused me to become a ghost in my afterlife and you also will become like this. It is the duty and the privilege of every man to wander forth among his fellow men making them happy, and if he goes not forth in life, he is doomed to do so after death, and witness what he might have shared of happiness, but cannot share,"

Everyone should share and make others happy, and if he can't, then after death, he has to suffer miserably. He becomes a source of other people's unhappiness instead of their happiness. So, if we don't make others happy, we'll become unhappy; if we make others happy, we'll become happy. It is a win-win for everybody. Scrooge practically wetted his nightgown thinking that he was going to become a green blob after death.

Then Marley disappeared and another ghost appeared. It was the ghost of the past Christmases. It showed Scrooge all the past Christmases that Scrooge had lived and hadn't done anything for anybody. In fact, he had made everybody miserable through his stinginess and selfishness. Then, still another ghost came. It was the ghost of the future Christmases, and he showed Scrooge all the possibilities that were still there for him in his life to make others happy and to become happy himself.

In that vision, there was one of Scrooge's employees named Bob. Bob was being terribly underpaid. His family was starving because of his lack of income, and he was being made to work even on Christmas Eve. He had a little boy, Tim, who was crippled in one leg and was about to die of starvation. They called him Tiny Tim because he was so under-fed. After seeing that, Scrooge woke up in an agitated state.

Sometimes we have a dream that is very clear, almost as clear as the waking state. It may be pleasant or painful, but it will be life changing. Such dreams cannot be ignored. Some may not be due to impressions of the waking state, but rather put in our mind by other beings—by our Guru, another mahatma, or even God.

Scrooge had a complete change of heart. He went running to the market and bought a lot of delicious, nourishing food, and took it to Bob's house. The family was afraid to open the door. They thought the fellow had come to beat them up or call them to his store for work. But he was crying and pleading to be let in, so they finally opened the door. He gave them the food and made everybody happy and Tiny Tim became healthy because of the nourishing food. After that, to everyone's amazement, Scrooge lost his former miserliness and became a great philanthropist.

The moral of the story is: miserliness won't make us happy. We might think that by safeguarding our possessions, we're going to be happy, but the truth is that it is not so. The tighter we embrace Maya, the more miserable we will become, and the deeper we will get involved in illusion. The farther we get from the real source of bliss—our True Nature, the expansive Self—the more our heart will dry up and we will become unhappy.

Have Desires That Lead to God

"Children, there is a great difference between the desires of a sadhak and those of a worldly person. Like waves, desires will come one after another and disturb the worldly man. There is no end to his desires. For a spiritual seeker, there is only one desire; once it is fulfilled, desire is no more."

Amma is saying that the nature of the mind is to desire. The moment we wake up, our mind gets separated from its blissful source, the Self, and the desire to recapture that bliss through worldly happiness arises. This is true for all living beings. We can never fully satisfy our desires. We need not get rid of desire. Amma is saying here that a sadhak also has a desire; but what desire? If we want to get rid of this illusory thing, this troublesome thing called "desire," which sometimes takes us in the wrong direction, we should use it, but in the right way. Desire something that is going to satisfy us when we get it.

If I get a new shirt or a new pair of shoes, I'm going to be happy for a little while, and then that goes away, and I get bored, and I want a new one. It may be food, music or anything. There is no end to that process because our desires are endless. We have infinite desires, infinite thirst for happiness. But the objects don't satisfy us. Desire is a bottomless pit. We go on putting things in it, and then, for a moment, it seems to be full, but soon enough, we need to fill it up again. So it is better to desire something that could permanently fill up that pit.

What can we fill up an infinite pit with? Infinity! We have to fill that infinite hole with something that is equally infinite, and then, that will be the end of the trouble. That is only the Divine, the Ocean of Bliss. There is no other solution.

After hearing a talk about Vedanta, someone said, "Wow, that really makes me look at life in a different way."

We can keep living. We can keep having our desires and enjoy as much as we want, but remember this point: don't jump into pleasure with so much relish. Temper it with the idea that however much I go for these things, I'm never going to be satisfied. I should also try for something that is infinite, something that is eternal. We may think, 'How are we to decide what is infinite and eternal? It is all hearsay. Just because some book says that there is an Infinite Being, how can we believe it? Are we going to give up all our sense happiness just because some book says so? No.'

We don't have to. However, what about the people that have experienced Divine Bliss? Those are the sages and saints of history. At present also, there are people who are experiencing Supreme Bliss, Self-realization. Those are our authorities. We should base our faith on what they say. Amma says that is where the real bliss is—the bliss of God-realization. Desire that, and in doing that, other lesser desires may come up. This is what Amma is talking about, the desires of a sadhak. For example, we do puja. Many of us do puja. We feel a special happiness when we're doing it. When we walk down the road and see some beautiful flowers in somebody's front yard, a desire comes to get those flowers to offer in our worship. That doesn't mean we should steal them; we can ask for them. Even better, we can grow our own flowers. It is a desire, but there is nothing wrong with that desire, because it is just supplementing or strengthening our big desire for God-realization. Or we may want to go on a pilgrimage to a holy place. We may want to go to visit a saint. We may want to read or buy a spiritual book. All these are desires. There is nothing wrong with them, because they're helping us get closer to the Truth, helping us reach the final satisfaction of God-realization.

Selfishness

This is what Amma means by the difference between a sadhak's desires and a worldly person's desires. And once it is fulfilled—a spiritual seeker's one big desire—then desire is no more. Once we realize God, once we attain union with God, then we're full. Then there is no more desire. That is Perfection. That is absolute satisfaction. That is Liberation.

> "The selfishness of a spiritual aspirant will be beneficial to the world. Once there were two boys in a village. Both of them received a seed from a sannyasi who came there. The first boy roasted the seed and ate it, appeasing his hunger. The second boy sowed the seed and thereby produced a lot of grain which he then distributed among others. Children, even though both boys had the selfishness to accept the seed, the selfishness of the second boy was beneficial to many people."

Everybody has their desires, and they accept the grace of God in various forms, but some people just satisfy themselves, while other people use the grace of God to become prosperous spiritually. Beyond the little circle of self or family, they make others happy also. A real sannyasi is a blessing to the whole world. They have nothing for themselves. They don't desire anything for themselves except God. In that process, they become so selfless that they become a source of happiness to everybody.

> "There is only one Atman. It is all-pervasive. When we become broad-minded, we can merge with It. Then selfishness and ego will disappear. Children, without wasting a single moment, serve others and help the destitute people. Without expecting anything from others, serve them."

There is one Intelligent Being pervading the whole universe. All of us are like waves on the ocean of the Paramatman. We're temporary. However, the thing that is real in us is eternal. That is awareness, and that is the Universal Being. The more we stress on our individuality, the farther we are from that Truth.

If a wave wants to become eternal, it has to sink into the ocean, and then it becomes the ocean itself. It doesn't cease to exist—it just expands to infinity at that moment. The ocean was always its substratum. It doesn't even exist apart from the ocean. But as long as it is sticking its head up above the water, it remains as a wave, and gets knocked here and there, and ultimately disappears. If the wave subsides, then what is left is the ocean. Amma is saying that by getting rid of selfishness and ego, one can be really happy, and one way is to broaden the mind and serve others. This is a practicable part of Amma's teaching. Serve others, especially people that really need something, either materially or spiritually. We should be useful to others.

Sometimes people who are interested in spiritual life go about this problem of gaining happiness through renunciation. They leave everything and meditate and do other kinds of spiritual practices. That is good, in that such practices deal with half of the problem—distraction. Nevertheless, the other half, the ego, may not decrease only by such disciplines. Unless one lives with a Realized Guru who will remove their egotism, their selfishness, they won't go very far. An advanced sadhak will have deep concentration as well as humility and compassion.

Eknath and the Donkey

One day, Eknath wanted to do a traditional kind of pilgrimage. For that, he would have to go to Benares, collect Ganges water in a pot, and carry that water all the way down to Rameshwaram at the southern tip of India. That is about 2400 kilometers (about 1500 miles) distance! There were hardly any roads. In fact, in those days, there were dense forests with tigers and other carnivorous animals. There were no hotels that one could go to for food. There might have been some villages where one could get something to eat. Maybe not, also. One was really at the mercy of God.

Eknath had a living faith in God's existence, and the very thought of carrying that water and using it to bathe the Sivalingam in Rameshwaram thrilled him and gave him the strength and courage to make the trip. It took him many months and a lot of hardship, but he finally reached Rameshwaram. When he was about a mile from the temple, he saw a donkey lying by the side of the road with its tongue hanging out, dying of thirst. Without even a second thought, he took the holy water, sat down besides the donkey, and poured all of it into its mouth. At that moment, he experienced the same happiness and satisfaction as if he had poured the water on the Shivalingam. He saved the life of the donkey. He saw God in the donkey.

He never considered devotion to God as higher than devotion to suffering beings. He always intuitively made the right choice because of his devotion. This is what Amma is saying, that selflessness and sharing is most important. Look at Amma's life. That is what her life has been from the beginning—constant sharing! She walks the talk and shows us also how to do it.

www.ingramcontent.com/pod-product-compliance
Lightning Source LLC
Chambersburg PA
CBHW060155050426
42446CB00013B/2830